Where's My Receipts?

How to Break Free from Confirmative Thinking

DR. TIFFINEE YANCEY

Published by: Virtual Peace of Mind Press
4897 Bennetts Pasture Rd. #5354 Suffolk, VA 23435

PN ISBN: 979-8-9993694-0-6
eBook ISBN: 979-8-9993694-1-3
Printed in the United States of America.

Dedication

To my parents, **Willis and Evelyn Anderton**,
who gave me my roots and foundation. You inspired me to
reach past the stars and share my experience with the world.

To my five incredible children—
DzJone, Kendra, Keyona, Alan, and Ryan—
your presence in my life continues to stretch me, ground me,
and grow me.

To my seven beautiful grandchildren—
**Taliyah, Tyaire, Ry'Neia, Asa, Ryelle, Zariyah, and
Zakai**—
you are living reminders that what we teach, model, and
believe echoes across generations.

And to **my most wonderful husband, Alan Singletary**,
whose love, encouragement, and unwavering support are the
RECEIPTS that are treasured most.
Thank you—for being my why.

Table of Contents

Introduction 6

Chapter 1: What Are Receipts, Anyway? 11

Chapter 2: The Brain's Default Mode: Confirmative Thinking 18

Chapter 3: Negative Stinkin' Thinkin' 28

Chapter 4: The Cost of Living Without Receipts 38

Chapter 5: The Road to Self-Deception... 54

Chapter 6: How to Find Your Receipts 68

Chapter 7: Turning Off the Overthinking Machine................................. 99

Chapter 8: The Power of Self-Reflection: Building Internal Receipts. 114

Chapter 9: External Receipts: Tying Together Internal & External Receipts.. 124

Chapter 10: Building Emotional Resilience Through Receipts 132

Chapter 11: The Balance Between Trust & Verification: When to Trust Your Gut 142

Chapter 12: The Power of Perspective....................................... 151

Chapter 13: The Practice of Validating Your Receipts 157

Conclusion: Moving Forward with Confidence..................................... 164

Fact vs. Opinion Worksheet 170

Mindful Journaling Worksheet 172

Cognitive Defusion Worksheet 174

Five-Minute Rule Worksheet 176

Journaling for Clarity & Insight Worksheet..178

Self-Questioning Worksheet..180

Gut Check Worksheet...182

Introduction

In a world overflowing with information, opinions, and instantaneous feedback, the line between what's true and what's simply believed has grown hazy. Facts and personal feelings often become entangled, creating a bubble in which people live by what they want to believe rather than what's objectively accurate. *Where's My Receipts?* is a guide to help you break free from the trap of confirmative thinking—the habit of reinforcing pre-existing beliefs without question. The book will equip you with tools to challenge your thoughts using evidence as opposed to assumptions, offering a path toward clear, grounded decision-making.

Essentially, a receipt serves as proof of a transaction. Just as a store receipt verifies a purchase, your "mental receipts" are evidence that your beliefs are rooted in objective truth. The title, *Where's My Receipts?*, symbolizes the importance of seeking out this evidence to support your beliefs and decisions, preventing you from getting lost in assumptions or emotional certainty.

Living in an Era of Assumptions

The need for receipt-based thinking is more urgent now than ever before. We live in a time in which misinformation spreads quickly and assumptions often masquerade as truth. Social media platforms, news outlets, and even our personal relationships can reinforce false beliefs, making it harder to discern what's real and what's not. In this environment, the ability to gather and verify receipts is a critical skill.

Every day, we're bombarded with information—some of it factual, but much of it not. It's easy to fall into the trap of believing things simply because they confirm what we already think, or because they fit into the narrative we want to be true.

But this approach leads to a narrow, skewed view of the world. It limits our ability to grow, to learn, and to make informed decisions. Receipt-based thinking is a way to combat this. It allows you to cut through the noise and focus on what's true, sharpening your ability to separate facts from distortions. This mental clarity becomes your compass in a world where the loudest voice often drowns out the most accurate one.

The Goal of *Where's My Receipts?*

The intention of this guide is simple: to teach you how to validate your beliefs and thoughts with objective truth. Whether you're dealing with personal relationships, career decisions, or even your own self-perception, it will help you develop the mental discipline needed to seek out facts before settling on a conclusion. It'll help you avoid the trap of making decisions based solely on feelings, assumptions, or incomplete information.

It isn't about teaching you to be skeptical of everything or to live in constant doubt. Rather, it's about helping you develop a healthy balance between trust and verification. It's about learning when to accept something as true and when to demand more proof. In a world where people often leap to conclusions without evidence—whether in politics, relationships, or personal self-worth—*Where's My Receipts?* will equip you with the tools to take a step back and ask, *"Where's the evidence that supports this belief?"* If there's no solid receipt, then it's time to dig deeper before accepting something as truth.

By consistently practicing receipt-based thinking, you build a foundation of confidence in your own judgment. Instead of second-guessing yourself, you'll know your choices are grounded in truth, which strengthens both your self-trust and your integrity.

The Pillars of Receipt-Based Thinking

The book is structured around three main pillars, each of which will guide you toward developing a mindset grounded in evidence and objectivity:

1. **Defining What Receipts Are**
   Before you can start collecting your receipts, you need to understand what qualifies. This section will help you distinguish between facts, opinions, and assumptions. You'll learn how to recognize when your thoughts are based on solid evidence and when they're merely the product of your emotions or biases. We'll explore the difference between objective facts (receipts) and subjective interpretations, and we'll look at how to apply this distinction in daily routines.

2. **The Consequences of Living Without Receipts**
   When you operate without receipts, you open yourself up to a range of negative consequences. This section will explore the mental, emotional, and relational toll that comes with living in a state of assumption rather than verification. We'll look at how unverified beliefs can lead to anxiety, overthinking, and self-doubt. We'll also explore how unchecked assumptions can damage your relationships and decision-making abilities. By understanding the costs of living without receipts, you'll gain a deeper appreciation for why it's so important to base your beliefs on objective evidence.

3. **Practicing the Skills of Validating Your Receipts**
   Practical tools and strategies are needed for you to properly gather and verify your receipts. You'll learn how to ask the right questions, where to find reliable sources of evidence, and how to challenge your own cognitive biases. How to apply receipt-based thinking in various areas of life, including personal relationships, career decisions, and self-perception is covered. By the

end of the book, you'll have a toolkit for ensuring that your thoughts, beliefs, and actions are based in truth.

How to Use This Book

Where's My Receipts? is designed to be both a guide and a practical workbook. Each chapter will provide you with insights and strategies for developing a receipt-based mindset, but the real transformation comes when you put these ideas into practice. Throughout these pages, you'll find exercises and reflective prompts that encourage you to apply receipt-based thinking in your own life. These exercises are designed to help you identify the areas where you tend to operate without receipts and to develop the skills needed to change that. The worksheet pages will be located at the end of the book.

It's important to approach this process with an open mind. Receipt-based thinking requires you to challenge your existing beliefs and be willing to accept that you may have been wrong about certain things. This can be uncomfortable at first, but it's also incredibly freeing. As you apply these tools, you'll see your relationships grow stronger because communication is based on facts, not assumptions. You'll approach conversations, decisions, and even disagreements with a steady mind, ready to listen, understand, and respond with fairness.

It isn't about perfection—it's about *progress*. The goal isn't to become someone who constantly doubts everything, but rather to become someone who has the mental discipline to seek out the truth, even when it's inconvenient or uncomfortable. By the time you finish *Where's My Receipts?*, you'll be equipped with the tools you need to make better decisions, avoid the pitfalls of cognitive distortions, and live a life grounded in objective truth.

In the following chapters, we'll delve deeper into these concepts, starting with a clear definition of what receipts are and how they differ from the assumptions and opinions we often mistake for truth. Let's begin your journey toward receipt-based thinking—toward living a life in which your beliefs are backed by facts, not just by what you *want* to believe.

Chapter 1: What Are Receipts, Anyway?

In this chapter, we define what we mean by "receipts" in the context of mental and emotional health. Receipts are the facts—objective truths—that support our beliefs, actions, and perceptions. Without them, our minds can drift into overthinking and self-deception.

When we talk about beliefs, thoughts, and decision-making, one of the most fundamental and often overlooked aspects is the concept of evidence—or, as we'll call it throughout the book, receipts. Just as you wouldn't leave a store without a receipt to prove your purchase, you shouldn't allow yourself to accept a thought or belief without evidence to back it up. But what exactly qualifies as a receipt when it comes to your beliefs? In this chapter, we'll break down the idea of receipts, explain how to identify them in different areas of your life, and explore why they're so essential in preventing the kind of thinking that can lead to self-deception, over-analysis, and negative spirals.

Facts vs. Opinions: Knowing the Difference

One of the most common traps people fall into is confusing their opinions or emotions for facts. While this may seem like a simple distinction on the surface, it's incredibly easy to blur the line between what is objectively true and what feels true in the moment. This is particularly relevant when emotions are involved, as emotions tend to cloud our judgment and make it more difficult to see the clear, evidence-based picture.

So, what exactly are facts, and how do they differ from opinions? A fact is an objective piece of information that can be verified independently of how you or anyone else feels about it. It's rooted in reality, and its truth can be tested by multiple people using standard methods. For example, if you say, "It's raining outside," that's a fact that anyone can verify by simply opening their front door or checking the weather report. Facts exist outside of your perceptions or interpretations—they just *are*.

On the other hand, an opinion is a personal interpretation of a fact. It's subjective, shaped by your experiences, feelings, and beliefs. "I hate the rain" is an opinion. Two people can look at the same rainy day, and one might feel gloomy while the other feels refreshed. The fact of rain itself remains unchanged regardless of how each person feels about it, but their opinions diverge based on their personal reactions.

A critical first step in gathering your mental receipts is developing the ability to distinguish between what's a fact and what's merely an opinion. This skill is essential because opinions, while valid in many contexts, don't qualify as receipts when it comes to decision-making or belief formation. Receipts must be rooted in objective truth, not in personal feelings or desires. Without that grounding, you're simply acting based on assumptions, which often leads to misunderstandings, poor choices, and unnecessary conflict.

Think about the assumptions you make in your regular interactions. Let's say you send a text to a friend, but they don't reply for hours. You might begin to form beliefs based on that delay. Maybe you think *"they're ignoring me"* or *"they must be mad at me"*. These are opinions, not facts. The fact is that your friend hasn't responded yet, but you don't have any verifiable evidence for why that is. The receipt would be an actual explanation from your friend—such as them telling you that they were busy or showing you that their phone was on silent. Without a receipt, you're left with assumptions that may or may not be true.

Understanding this distinction is crucial because it allows you to question the narratives you create in your mind and ask, *"Where's the receipt for this belief?"* If you can't find a fact-based piece of evidence to support your thought, it may be time to reconsider it.

To help you build this skill in real time, let's put this concept into practice. The following exercise will guide you through a hands-on process of breaking down a belief you've recently held—so you can clearly see where the facts end, and the opinions begin. This is your chance to practice thinking like a receipt-checker, training your mind to pause and evaluate instead of react and assume.

Exercise: Fact vs. Opinion Worksheet

- **Purpose**: To learn how to differentiate between facts and opinions in your daily thoughts and decisions.
- **Activity**: Choose a recent belief you've been holding and break it down into its factual components and opinion-based components. Then answer the following:
    o *What are the facts?*
    o *What are my opinions about this situation?*
    o *How can I verify the facts?*

By separating what's real from what you feel, you begin to build a habit of mental accountability—grounding your beliefs in truth, not just perception. This shift isn't just helpful in analyzing past events; it's crucial when making decisions that impact your future.

Receipts in Personal Decisions: Testing Your Assumptions

Now that we've established the importance of distinguishing facts from opinions, let's apply this concept to personal decision-making. One of the most common areas where people fail to gather receipts is in the assumptions they make about themselves and their abilities. This often leads to limiting beliefs, where you convince yourself you're incapable of achieving something without ever questioning whether that belief is based on fact.

Consider a situation in which you're contemplating applying for a new job. The job listing includes a variety of qualifications, some of which you feel confident about and others you're unsure of. As you read through the list, you begin to doubt yourself. You think, *"I'm not qualified for this"*. But where's the receipt? Do you have concrete evidence that you lack the necessary skills, or is that just your opinion?

Your receipt in this case could come from several sources. You might look at your résumé and compare it directly to the job requirements. Do you meet most of the criteria? If so, your self-doubt might not be based on facts. Another potential receipt could come from feedback you've received from colleagues or mentors. Have they praised your abilities in the areas you're questioning? If so, that's evidence that you're more qualified than you initially thought. Conversely, if you look at the job listing and realize that you're missing key qualifications that can't be overlooked, that's also a receipt—it's a fact that you're not yet ready for that specific role, and you can make a plan to gain those skills.

What's important here is that you're not relying solely on feelings but actively gathering facts that confirm or challenge your belief. Without them, decisions risk being driven by fear, insecurity, or false confidence.

This approach can be applied to almost any personal decision, whether it's regarding your career, relationships, or personal growth. In each case, ask yourself: *"What evidence do I have to support this belief? What facts can I point to that confirm or challenge the assumptions I'm making?"* If you don't have a receipt, you don't have a solid foundation for making that decision.

The Role of Evidence: Receipts Must Be Verifiable

When we talk about receipts, one of the most important aspects is that they must be verifiable. This means your evidence should be something others can independently check or confirm, regardless of personal feelings. Why is this so crucial? Because human beings have a natural tendency to seek out information that confirms what they already believe—a phenomenon known as *confirmation bias*.

Confirmation bias is the mental habit of focusing on evidence that supports your pre-existing beliefs while ignoring or downplaying evidence that contradicts them. This is why it's so important to gather receipts that can stand up to scrutiny. If your receipt is something that only makes sense in your own mind or is based on highly subjective experiences, it's not truly a receipt—it's just another opinion disguised as fact.

Let's say you're convinced that your coworker dislikes you. Maybe you've noticed them avoiding eye contact or not engaging with you in meetings. These are observations, but they don't necessarily qualify as receipts. They could be explained by a variety of factors—you don't know for sure that your coworker's behavior is related to their feelings toward you. To gather your receipt, you might need to ask for direct feedback or observe more concrete actions that can't be explained away by other factors. Think about, if your coworker makes a negative comment about you to someone else, that's a verifiable receipt. It's a fact that can be confirmed by others.

The point here is that receipts must be based on reality, not assumptions or interpretations. When you base your beliefs on verifiable evidence, you protect yourself from falling into the trap of confirmation bias. Instead of only seeing what you want to see, you open yourself up to the full picture, even if that picture isn't what you hoped for.

In some cases, gathering receipts requires you to seek out information from external sources. For example, if you're unsure about a medical diagnosis, you might seek a second opinion from another doctor to verify the accuracy of the first diagnosis. Or if you're making a major financial decision, you might consult a financial advisor to confirm that your plans are sound. In both cases, the goal is to gather receipts that are grounded in expert knowledge and can be independently verified.

The more verifiable receipts you collect, the stronger the foundation for your beliefs. Without them, you're building your mental framework on shaky ground, prone to collapse when faced with challenges or contradictions.

Emotional Receipts: Are Your Feelings Grounded in Reality?

One of the most challenging areas to apply the concept of receipts is in the realm of emotions. Emotions are powerful, and they can often feel like irrefutable truth. When you feel something strongly, it's easy to assume that the feeling itself is all the proof you need. But emotions, while valid and important, don't always reflect objective reality. In fact, they can sometimes *distort* your perception of reality, leading you to believe things that aren't true.

That's why it's essential to gather emotional receipts—evidence that your feelings are grounded in facts rather than assumptions or misinterpretations. This doesn't mean invalidating your emotions or dismissing them as irrelevant. Instead, it means taking a step back and asking, *"Is there evidence to support this feeling?"* or *"What facts are contributing to my emotional response?"*

Imagine you're feeling upset because you believe a family member intentionally missed your birthday party. Your emotion is valid in the sense that it's your real, lived experience—you genuinely feel hurt. But before you act on that feeling, it's important to check whether your emotional response is based on facts. Did your family member deliberately avoid the party, or could there be other explanations for their absence? Maybe they've been unwell, or perhaps they're dealing with a personal issue that has nothing to do with you. In this case, the receipt would be a clear pattern of behavior showing that the family member has been distancing themselves from you.

As we begin to understand the importance of receipts in our decision-making, it's essential to acknowledge the role our brain plays in shaping our beliefs. While it's natural to seek out information that confirms what we already believe, this tendency can lead us astray. In the next chapter, we'll examine how the brain's default mode of confirmative thinking works, and how it can impact our ability to make clear and objective decisions.

Chapter 2: The Brain's Default Mode: Confirmative Thinking

Humans are wired to seek out information that confirms what we already believe. It's comforting—but it can also be misleading. Instead of seeking truth, we often unconsciously favor information that reinforces our current perspective. In this chapter, we'll explore the phenomenon of confirmative thinking and why our brains instinctively filter out evidence that challenges our beliefs.

Human beings are natural storytellers—from the earliest days of civilization, we've used stories to interpret complex realities, assign meaning to events, and create a sense of coherence. But this tendency to seek patterns and explanations has a downside. Instead of actively searching for the truth, we often unconsciously look for evidence that supports our existing perspective.

This is the essence of confirmative thinking: our brain's default mode of processing information in a way that reinforces what we *want* to be true rather than what's *objectively* accurate. We filter the world through a lens shaped by our existing beliefs, selectively noticing what supports those beliefs and ignoring anything that contradicts them. This mental shortcut is comforting—but it distorts our perception and limits our ability to grow, learn, and make better decisions.

To understand why this bias is so persistent, we need to explore its psychological roots. Why does the brain favor confirmation over truth? What purpose did this serve in our evolution? And more importantly, how can we learn to challenge it today? This chapter explores how confirmative thinking shapes our minds—and how we can break free from its grip to live with greater clarity and intention.

Why the Brain Favors Confirmation

At its core, confirmation bias developed as a survival mechanism. In early human history, our ancestors had to make quick decisions in dangerous environments. Whether it was determining if a plant was poisonous or assessing whether someone was a threat, the brain relied on fast pattern recognition drawn from past experience. Hesitating or overanalyzing could mean death.

To stay safe, the brain learned to prioritize evidence that supported existing beliefs—like remembering that a certain plant made someone sick—while ignoring contradictory outcomes. It was more efficient (and safer) to stick with what had worked before, even if that meant missing occasional exceptions.

Today, our brains still use this shortcut—but the challenges we face are about relationships, careers, finances, and identity rather than survival. We're no longer navigating life-or-death situations every day. Instead, we're making decisions about relationships, emotions, careers, and identity. Yet the brain still seeks out what confirms what we already think, not necessarily what's true. This outdated habit can lead us to cling to harmful or inaccurate beliefs simply because they're easier to process.

In today's information-saturated world, the brain filters and prioritizes what aligns with our worldview—because it takes less mental energy. But this ease comes at a cost: it narrows our perspective and reinforces what we already believe, even when that belief isn't helpful or true.

This is why confirmation bias is so powerful. It's not a flaw in reasoning—it's an ancient mental habit that once helped us survive. But in today's world, it can stand in the way of growth, connection, and clarity.

The Role of Emotions in Confirmative Thinking

Emotions powerfully shape our perceptions, especially when we're caught in confirmative thinking. Strong feelings—whether joy, anger, fear, or sadness—color how we interpret the world. Instead of evaluating facts, we often amplify information that matches our emotional state and filter out what doesn't. This emotional filtering doesn't just reinforce our thoughts—it deepens our beliefs.

Imagine a time when you felt upset—perhaps a friend made a comment that stung, or your boss criticized a project you worked hard on. In that moment, your mind likely began racing, recalling past experiences that supported your frustration while ignoring moments of kindness or support.

The same works in reverse. When you're feeling good, you're more likely to notice what's going well, overlook small irritations, and assume good intentions. Our emotional state doesn't just shape our mood—it affects what we believe to be true, creating a feedback loop that reinforces whatever emotion we start with.

That's how emotions amplify confirmative thinking. When we're upset, we naturally search for evidence that supports the emotional narrative we're living. Even neutral or positive events can be reinterpreted as negative when viewed through that lens—and the same is true of positive emotions. When we're in a good mood, we're more likely to notice uplifting things, give others the benefit of the doubt, and overlook small mistakes. Our emotions shape how we see the world—not just in the moment, but in how we remember, react, and reinforce our beliefs over time.

Emotional Reasoning vs. Objective Reasoning

Emotional reasoning occurs when we assume something is true simply because we feel it intensely. The stronger the feeling, the more believable the narrative becomes—even if the facts tell a different story.

Consider preparing for a big presentation. Despite your preparation and past success, anxiety creeps in. Emotional reasoning may convince you that you're bound to fail—not because of evidence, but because the anxiety feels so real.

Objective reasoning challenges this by asking us to pause and examine the evidence. It doesn't ignore your emotions but seeks verification. In this case, objective reasoning would prompt you to review your notes, recall positive feedback, or ask a colleague for input—grounding your thinking in facts rather than fear.

The Feedback Loop Between Feelings & Beliefs

Emotions and beliefs often create a reinforcing cycle. What we believe shapes how we feel—and how we feel reinforces what we believe. This feedback loop can become self-perpetuating, especially when left unchecked.

For example, if you're in a new relationship and feel insecure, you might believe your partner is not as invested. That belief fuels anxiety. Then, you interpret neutral actions—like a missed call—as proof that something is wrong. Anxiety deepens your belief, and the belief heightens your emotional response.

Breaking this loop starts with seeking receipts—objective evidence that supports or refutes your belief. In a relationship, this might mean having a direct conversation with your partner, asking clear questions, listening to their perspective, and reflecting on patterns of behavior over time.

Recognizing the Patterns of Confirmative Thinking

Confirmative thinking is so deeply embedded in our thought processes that it often runs unnoticed in the background. But with awareness and intention, it becomes possible to recognize these patterns and interrupt them before they take hold. The first step is learning to spot the warning signs.

One clear sign is when you're focusing only on information that supports your existing belief while ignoring or dismissing anything that contradicts it. This kind of selective filtering can show up in both personal and professional settings.

Imagine you've formed a negative opinion about a colleague—you've decided they're unreliable. From that point on, you begin to notice every late arrival or missed deadline. These incidents reinforce your belief. Meanwhile, moments when they deliver great work or contribute above expectations tend to fade into the background. You're not seeing the full picture—just the version that supports your narrative.

Another red flag is the unwillingness to consider alternative explanations. When we're caught in a confirmation loop, we often dismiss or minimize new information without fair consideration. This can sound like a quick, "That's not true," or a reflexive assumption that someone's opposing view must be wrong simply because it challenges what we already think.

Real-Life Traps: Where Confirmation Bias Hides

Confirmative thinking can show up in everyday life, often without us realizing it. Below are some common areas where it tends to take hold—along with signs that your brain might be filtering for evidence instead of truth.

- In *relationships*, you may begin to believe your relationship is on shaky grounds. After a rough day, if your partner seems distant, your mind might jump to the conclusion that they're upset with you. You mentally replay the week, searching for "evidence," while overlooking other explanations like stress or fatigue. Convinced something's wrong, you grow defensive, and tension builds. This reaction stems not from facts, but from unchecked beliefs. The solution is simple yet powerful: ask—don't assume.
- In the workplace, confirmative thinking can quietly shape how individuals are perceived—and how they perceive themselves. Imagine a manager who believes one employee is less competent. Every misstep becomes proof, while success is brushed off. Over time, the employee may internalize this perception, which harms performance, morale, and team trust. When feedback and recognition are filtered through bias, innovation suffers and collaboration stalls.
- On social media, the effects of confirmative thinking are amplified. Platforms like Facebook, Instagram, and X (formerly Twitter) track what you click and engage with, then serve you more of the same. Over time, your feed can become a personalized echo chamber that continually reinforces your existing beliefs while filtering out opposing views. This dynamic can distort your sense of reality, reduce critical thinking, and heighten polarization. Conversations become debates. Disagreement feels like disrespect. And we instinctively dismiss anything that doesn't align with what we already think.

The Consequences of Unchecked Confirmative Thinking

When confirmative thinking goes unchecked, it can affect every area of life—mental health, relationships, and decision-making. One of the most damaging effects is its ability to trap us in negative thinking loops. If you believe you're not good enough, your mind will constantly search for "evidence" to support that belief—mistakes, criticism, or rejection. Meanwhile, it will ignore encouragement, success, or compliments.

This pattern can lead to increased anxiety, low self-esteem, and even depression. We begin to believe our fears and insecurities are facts, and we shape our lives around them. The same thing happens in relationships. You might misread someone's silence as anger, or assume their distraction is disinterest—when in reality, they're just tired or stressed. Misunderstandings grow. Defensiveness builds. Communication shuts down.

Confirmative thinking can also distort decision-making. You might stick with a business idea, a relationship, or a health belief, not because it's wise—but because it confirms what you already hope to be true. We prioritize what feels familiar over what's accurate. That's the danger: not just that we're wrong, but that we're *comfortable* being wrong.

The hardest part? This mental habit often keeps us from developing self-awareness. We avoid truths that might challenge our identity or force us to change. We tell ourselves we're right. We shift blame. We double down. But clarity only comes when we're willing to ask: *"Where's the evidence for this belief?"* If the answer is missing—it might be time to let that belief go.

The Cognitive Biases That Stem from Confirmative Thinking

Confirmative thinking is closely linked to several cognitive biases—mental shortcuts our brains use to simplify complex decisions. While these shortcuts can be efficient, they often lead us away from objectivity. Below are three key biases that commonly emerge from confirmative thinking:

Availability Bias. We tend to make judgments based on information that's most readily available to us, not necessarily what's most accurate. For instance, after hearing several news stories about plane crashes, you may begin to overestimate the likelihood of a crash on your upcoming flight—even though statistically, flying remains extremely safe. Because these vivid stories are fresh in your mind, they carry more weight than they deserve.

Anchoring Bias. This occurs when the first piece of information we encounter becomes the "anchor" for all future judgments. Say you're negotiating a salary, and the first offer is far lower than expected. Even if you're worth more, that initial figure can subconsciously lower your expectations and influence your final decision more than it should.

Confirmation Bias. This bias, at the core of confirmative thinking, is the tendency to seek out evidence that supports our preexisting beliefs while ignoring or dismissing anything that contradicts them. It limits our ability to make balanced decisions by cutting off opposing viewpoints before they're fully considered.

All of these biases reinforce our comfort zone, not necessarily our clarity. The more aware we are of these mental habits, the better equipped we are to challenge them—and make decisions grounded in truth rather than convenience.

How Confirmative Thinking Impacts Financial, Professional & Personal Choices

Confirmative thinking shows up in every area of life— especially when it comes to decisions involving money, career, and relationships.

Financially, it often leads to overconfidence. You might become convinced a particular investment will succeed and disregard market warnings or expert advice. You may pour more money into a strategy that feels promising—but isn't backed by fact.

Professionally, confirmative thinking can lock you into a narrow view of success. If you believe only one path or job title will make you happy, you may overlook opportunities that are a better fit. Bias thinking can also shape how you interpret feedback, collaboration, and leadership—limiting your potential to grow.

Personally, confirmative thinking often drives how we approach health and relationships. You might cling to a workout or diet plan that isn't working—just because it aligns with what you believe "should" work. Or, in a relationship, you may assume someone's silence means disinterest, while ignoring their other signals of care. These blind spots limit connection and clarity.

How Challenging Confirmative Thinking Changes Everything

The good news? You can challenge confirmative thinking— and when you do, you unlock better decision-making in every area of life.

Start by gathering receipts: objective evidence that either confirms or challenges your belief. If you're considering a career change, for example, that might mean talking with people who've made similar moves, researching job trends, and honestly assessing your skills. The goal isn't to talk yourself out of your instincts—it's to test them.

In financial decisions, this might involve seeking expert input, comparing strategies, or slowing down before committing. In doing so, you avoid the trap of selective attention and open yourself to wiser, longer-term outcomes.

In relationships, gathering receipts might look like asking clarifying questions, listening without interrupting, or checking whether your assumptions match the other person's reality. This approach strengthens communication and builds trust.

By taking the extra step to ask, *"What do I actually know to be true?"* you shift from reacting to reflecting. And that's where better choices begin.

Having explored how confirmative thinking forms, functions, and influences our lives, we're now ready to examine what happens when these unchecked beliefs spiral out of control. In the next chapter, we'll dive into what I call *"negative stinkin' thinkin'"*—the toxic, looping thoughts that take hold when we don't verify what we believe. You'll learn how to spot these patterns, understand their emotional cost, and break free before they pull you under.

Chapter 3: Negative Stinkin' Thinkin'

When our beliefs lack solid evidence, they can spiral into what I call negative stinkin' thinkin'—convincing ourselves the worst will happen without any real proof.

Our minds are incredibly powerful. They have the ability to create, to analyze, and to solve complex problems. But they also have a tendency to get stuck in negative thinking patterns, or negative stinkin' thinkin'. This mental trap can take many forms: ruminating over past mistakes, obsessing about worst-case scenarios, or allowing small setbacks to snowball into overwhelming crises. When left unchecked, negative stinkin' thinkin' can lead to anxiety, depression, and a general sense of dissatisfaction with life.

In this chapter, we're going to explore the mechanics of negative stinkin' thinkin'. We'll examine why it happens, how it affects our mental and emotional health, and, most importantly, how to break free from it. The goal is to help you recognize the patterns of negative thinking before they take over and to develop strategies for shifting your mindset toward a more balanced, evidence-based way of thinking.

What Is Negative Stinkin' Thinkin'?

Negative stinkin' thinkin' is exactly what it sounds like: it's when your mind gets stuck in a loop of negative thoughts, and you can't seem to break free. These thoughts often start small— maybe you're worried about an upcoming meeting at work or replaying an awkward conversation with a friend. But instead of resolving these concerns, your mind keeps going over them repeatedly, making the situation seem bigger and more threatening than it actually is.

Over time, negative stinkin' thinkin' can snowball. What starts as a small worry can turn into a major source of anxiety. Consider, if you're worried about hosting a community event, you might start imagining everything that could go wrong. You might picture yourself losing track of what you planned to say, forgetting important details, or sensing disapproval from attendees. The more you dwell on these possibilities, the more your anxiety builds—until the idea of standing in front of the group feels overwhelming.

This is the essence of negative stinkin' thinkin'. It's the mental habit of focusing on worst-case scenarios, magnifying small problems, and letting negative thoughts take on a life of their own. And while it's natural to have some degree of worry or concern in challenging situations, negative stinkin' thinkin' takes it to an unhealthy level where it starts to interfere with your ability to think clearly and act effectively.

The Science Behind Negative Stinkin' Thinkin'

To understand why negative stinkin' thinkin' happens, we need to take a closer look at the brain. The human brain is wired for survival, and one of its primary functions is to keep us safe from danger. This means that the brain is constantly scanning the environment for potential threats, and when it perceives one— whether it's a real, immediate danger or a perceived emotional threat (like criticism, rejection, or uncertainty), the brain often reacts the same way.

This response is often referred to as the "fight or flight" reaction, and it's controlled by a part of the brain called the *amygdala*. When the amygdala senses danger, it sends out signals that prepare the body to either confront the threat (fight) or escape from it (flight). This response served our ancestors well when they were facing physical dangers like predators or hostile environments. But in the modern world, most of the threats we face are psychological rather than physical. Unfortunately, the brain doesn't always make this distinction.

When you're stuck in negative stinkin' thinkin', your brain is essentially treating your worries as threats. The amygdala activates, sending out signals that keep you in a heightened state of alertness. This is why negative thoughts can feel so overwhelming—they're triggering the same biological response as if you were facing a physical threat. Because the brain is so focused on avoiding threats, it's much easier to fixate on negative possibilities than positive ones.

In addition to the amygdala, another part of the brain—the *prefrontal cortex*—plays a key role in negative stinkin' thinkin'. The prefrontal cortex is responsible for higher-level thinking, such as decision-making, problem-solving, and regulating emotions. In a healthy state, the prefrontal cortex works in harmony with the amygdala, helping to manage emotional responses and keep them in check. However, when negative stinkin' thinkin' takes over, the amygdala can hijack the prefrontal cortex, making it difficult to think rationally or see the bigger picture.

The Role of Cognitive Biases in Negative Stinkin' Thinkin'

Negative stinkin' thinkin' is closely linked to several cognitive biases—mental shortcuts that influence how we process information and make decisions. These biases can distort our thinking, making negative thoughts seem more plausible or important than they actually are. Below are some key cognitive biases or distortions that contribute to negative stinkin' thinkin':

- **Catastrophizing:** This is the tendency to assume that the worst possible outcome will happen. When you catastrophize, you take a small problem and blow it out of proportion, imagining that it will lead to a disaster. Let's say, you miss a family gathering, you might immediately assume everyone will be upset with you, even if the absence was unavoidable.

- **Confirmation Bias:** As mentioned previously, this reflects the inclination to seek out information that confirms what you already believe. In the case of negative stinkin' thinkin', confirmation bias can lead you to focus on any evidence that supports your negative thoughts while ignoring or dismissing evidence that contradicts them. If you're convinced that you're going to fail a test, you might only focus on the questions you got wrong in your practice exams and ignore the ones you got right.

- **Black-and-White Thinking:** This refers to seeing things in extremes, without recognizing the shades of gray in between. When you're stuck in black-and-white thinking, you might view situations as either completely good or completely bad, with no middle ground. Such as, if you receive one piece of critical feedback on an event, you might conclude that the entire event is a failure, even if most of the feedback was positive.

- **Overgeneralization:** This means applying a single negative experience to all future situations. If you have a bad first date, you might conclude that all future dates will go just as poorly, or if you fail at one task, you might assume that you'll fail at everything you try.

These cognitive biases can make it difficult to break free from negative stinkin' thinkin' because they reinforce the negative thought patterns that keep you stuck. However, by learning to recognize these biases, you can start to challenge them and shift your thinking in a more balanced direction.

The Consequences of Negative Stinkin' Thinkin'

Negative stinkin' thinkin' doesn't just affect your mental and emotional state—it can also have real-world consequences. Let's look at some ways that illustrate how getting stuck in negative thinking patterns can impact your life:

- **Increased Anxiety and Stress:** When you're constantly focused on worst-case scenarios, your body remains in a heightened state of alertness, which can lead to chronic apprehension and worry. Over time, this can take a toll on your physical health, contributing to issues like headaches, muscle tension, and digestive problems.

- **Reduced Problem-Solving Ability:** When you're stuck in negative stinkin' thinkin', it's difficult to think clearly or come up with effective solutions to problems. Instead of seeing the situation objectively, you become fixated on the negative aspects, which makes it harder to take action or move forward.

- **Relationship Strain:** Negative stinkin' thinkin' can also affect your relationships. If you fixate on potential conflicts—such as assuming someone is upset without confirming it—you may misinterpret neutral behaviors as personal slights. Over time, this can create unnecessary tension, prompting you to withdraw, become defensive, or grow overly critical. Left unchecked, these patterns can slowly erode trust and connection.

- **Decreased Motivation and Productivity:** When you're stuck in a loop of negative thinking, it can be difficult to find the motivation to take action. You might start to believe that your efforts won't make a difference, which can lead to procrastination or giving up on goals altogether.

- **Depression:** Over time, chronic negative stinkin' thinkin' can contribute to feelings of serious despair. When you're constantly focused on negative thoughts, it's hard to feel hopeful or optimistic about the future. This can create a downward spiral in which negative thoughts lead to negative feelings, which in turn reinforce the negative thoughts.

Recognizing Negative Stinkin' Thinkin' in Yourself

The first step to overcoming negative stinkin' thinkin' is recognizing when it's happening. This can be challenging because negative thinking often feels automatic—it's just the way your brain responds to certain situations. However, by becoming more aware of your thought patterns, you can start to notice when your mind is getting stuck in negativity and take steps to shift your thinking.

Below are several signs that you might be caught in negative stinkin' thinkin':

- **You're Ruminating:** Rumination is the habit of going over the same negative thoughts again and again, without finding a resolution. If you find yourself constantly replaying a past mistake or worrying about a future event, you might be caught in a loop of negative stinkin' thinkin'.
- **You're Catastrophizing:** If you often find yourself imagining the worst possible outcome in a situation, even when it's unlikely to happen, this is a sign that you're engaging in negative stinkin' thinkin'. Such as, if you're worried about an upcoming job interview, you might start to imagine that you'll completely bomb the meeting, not get the job, and end up unemployed forever.
- **You're Focusing on the Negative:** If you tend to zero in on the negative aspects of a situation while ignoring the positive, you might be stuck in negative stinkin' thinkin'. Let's say, you receive mostly positive feedback on a project but can't stop thinking about the one piece of criticism, this is a sign that your mind is fixating on the negative.
- **You're Engaging in "What If" Thinking:** This is when you constantly worry about hypothetical scenarios that

haven't happened yet—and might *never* happen. You might think, *What if I say something stupid in the meeting?* or *What if everyone hates my idea?* This type of thinking keeps you stuck in a loop of anxiety as your brain searches for potential threats to worry about.

- **You're Feeling Helpless or Hopeless:** Negative stinkin' thinkin' often leads to feelings of helplessness or hopelessness, as you start to believe that things will never improve. If you find yourself thinking, *What's the point?* or *Nothing ever works out for me*, this is a sign that negative stinkin' thinkin' has taken over.

Breaking Free from Negative Stinkin' Thinkin'

Once you've recognized that you're caught in negative stinkin' thinkin', the next step is to take action to break free from it. This can be challenging, especially if negative thinking has become a habit, but with practice, it's possible to shift your mindset and develop healthier thinking patterns.

Let's explore some strategies to help you break free from negative stinkin' thinkin':

- **Challenge Your Thoughts:** One of the most effective ways to combat negative stinkin' thinkin' is to confront your negative thoughts and question whether they're based on facts or assumptions. Ask yourself, *what evidence do I have to support this thought? Is there another way to interpret the situation?* By gathering receipts—objective evidence—you can start to see the situation more clearly and recognize when your negative thoughts are exaggerated or unfounded.

  Case in point, if you're worried about not getting a promotion, you might challenge your negative thoughts by reminding yourself of your past successes at work or seeking feedback from a colleague who believes in your abilities. By gathering receipts, you can start to shift your focus from worst-case scenarios to a more balanced perspective.

- **Practice Mindfulness:** Mindfulness is the practice of staying present in the moment without getting caught up in your thoughts or judgments. When you're stuck in negative stinkin' thinkin', mindfulness can help you step back from your thoughts and observe them without getting swept away by them. This can create space for you to respond to situations more calmly and rationally rather than reacting automatically to negative thoughts.

  To practice mindfulness, try paying attention to your breath or the sensations in your body. When negative thoughts arise, notice them without judgment and then gently bring your attention back to the present moment. Over time, mindfulness can help you become more aware of your thought patterns and create a buffer between your thoughts and your emotional reactions.

- **Reframe Your Thoughts:** Reframing is the process of shifting your perspective on a situation to see it in a more positive or balanced light. This doesn't mean ignoring or dismissing negative aspects of a situation—it simply means recognizing that there are multiple ways to interpret the same event and choosing to focus on the aspects that are more empowering or constructive.

  Imagine that you're feeling anxious about meeting your partner's family for the first time. You might reframe your thoughts by focusing on the opportunity to learn more about them and share who you are, rather than fixating on the possibility of saying something awkward or making a poor impression. Or, if you receive critical feedback at work, you might reframe it as a chance to improve and develop new skills rather than as a sign of incompetence.

- **Set Boundaries with Negative Thinking:** While it's impossible to completely eliminate negative thoughts, you can define limits and parameters to prevent them from taking over your mind. One way to do this is to set aside a specific time each day to focus on your worries or concerns. Let's say, you might schedule 15 minutes in the evening to think about any challenges or negative thoughts that have come up during the day. Outside of that time, whenever a negative thought arises, remind yourself that you'll deal with it during your designated "worry time."

This technique can help you avoid ruminating on negative thoughts throughout the day and create a sense of control over your thinking. By setting boundaries with your negative thoughts, you can create space for more positive or productive thinking.

- **Take Action:** Negative stinkin' thinkin' often keeps us stuck in a state of indecision or inaction as we become paralyzed by our worries or fears. One of the best ways to break free from this is to take action, even if it's a small step. Action helps shift your focus from your negative thoughts to the task at hand, and it can provide a sense of accomplishment and momentum.

An example would be, if you're feeling overwhelmed by a project at work, break it down into smaller tasks and start with the easiest one. Or if you're worried about a difficult conversation with a friend, take the first step by sending them a message to set up a time to talk. By taking action, you interrupt the cycle of negative thinking and start to move forward.

How to Break Free from Confirmative Thinking

Negative stinkin' thinkin' is a common mental trap, but it doesn't have to control your life. By becoming aware of your thought patterns, challenging your negative thoughts, and developing healthier thinking habits, you can break free from the cycle of negativity and create a more balanced mindset. This doesn't mean eliminating all negative thoughts—it means learning to see them for what they are: *thoughts, not facts*. With practice, you can develop the mental resilience to navigate challenges with clarity and confidence rather than getting stuck in a loop of negative thinking.

As you continue to build your receipt-based mindset, remember that the goal isn't to avoid all negative experiences or emotions—it's to approach them with curiosity, compassion, and objectivity. By gathering receipts and shifting your focus from worst-case scenarios to evidence-based thinking, you can create a mental environment that supports growth, well-being, and resilience.

Once we identify the trap of negative stinkin' thinkin', we need to recognize the cost of living without solid evidence to back up our beliefs. In the next chapter, we'll examine the profound consequences of making decisions based on assumptions rather than verified receipts. These consequences stretch far beyond mental health, affecting everything from our relationships to our professional lives, and we'll see how the ripple effect can be damaging.

Chapter 4: The Cost of Living Without Receipts

Believing what you want to believe—without evidence—can carry serious emotional, psychological, and social consequences. This chapter explores those outcomes in depth, helping you understand why it's so important to validate your thoughts.

In earlier chapters, we explored how our brains are wired for confirmative thinking, how negative stinkin' thinkin' can trap us in cycles of anxiety and doubt, and how these patterns distort our perception of reality.

Ultimately, living without receipts is costly—plain and simple. It affects every aspect of your life: your personal relationships, professional success, mental health, and even your physical well-being. Without receipts, your life is driven by a combination of assumptions, unchecked emotions, and biased perceptions that can lead to poor decision-making, damaged relationships, and an increased sense of insecurity and stress.

By the end of this chapter, you'll have a deeper understanding of the price you pay for living without evidence-based thinking, as well as the tools to recognize when you're falling into that pattern and how to change course. The cost of living without receipts is steep—but by recognizing and addressing it, you can avoid the pitfalls and set yourself on a path toward clarity, confidence, and grounded decision-making.

The Ripple Effect of Living Without Receipts

To understand the full impact of not basing our thoughts on objective reality, it's important to recognize how this habit ripples through various areas of life. When you make decisions or form beliefs without receipts, the effects are rarely contained to just one area. Instead, as mentioned previously, they tend to spill over into other domains, creating a domino effect that can disrupt your relationships, career, health, and overall sense of self-worth. Below, we'll examine each area in depth and illustrate just how detrimental living without an evidence-based mindset can be.

Relationships: Doubts & Insecurities

As mentioned back in Chapter 2, living without receipts can place an enormous strain on your relationships, which thrive on trust, communication, and mutual understanding. But when you operate on assumptions rather than facts, you introduce confusion, frustration, and conflict.

Let's take a common example: you send a message to a friend, and they don't reply for several hours. Without receipts, your mind might begin to fill in the gaps with all sorts of explanations: *they're mad at me, they don't care about our friendship anymore,* or *they're ignoring me on purpose.* None of these assumptions are based on actual evidence—yet the more you dwell on them, the more real they start to feel. By the time your friend responds with a simple, *"Sorry, I was busy at work,"* you may have already worked yourself into a state of frustration or hurt based entirely on assumptions.

This dynamic can play out in much larger, more significant ways in long-term relationships—especially romantic partnerships. If you believe that your partner is losing interest or doesn't care about you as much as you care about them, you might start interpreting their every action (or inaction) through that lens. A missed phone call becomes 'proof' they're disengaged. A short conversation before bed turns into "evidence" they no longer value your time together. Without clear, evidence-based communication—your receipts—these interpretations can spiral into resentment, mistrust, and unnecessary conflict.

Living without receipts in relationships leads to a constant undercurrent of doubt and insecurity. You find yourself questioning the other person's intentions, misinterpreting their actions, and, in turn, reacting in ways that can further strain the relationship. When both parties are operating on assumptions rather than clarity, the result is often misunderstanding, emotional distance, and a weakening of the bond that holds the relationship together.

Professional Life: Poor Decision-Making & Missed Opportunities

In the workplace, decisions are made every day that impact your career trajectory, your relationships with colleagues, and your overall job satisfaction. When those decisions are based on assumptions rather than evidence, the results can be costly.

Suppose you're offered a new position at work but hesitate because you believe you're not qualified. This belief might be based on feelings of self-doubt or imposter syndrome rather than on an objective assessment of your skills and qualifications. Without gathering receipts—such as seeking feedback from colleagues, reviewing your past achievements, or even looking at the job description more closely—you might turn down the opportunity, believing that you're not capable of handling the responsibilities. In doing so, you've potentially passed up a career advancement based on a feeling rather than fact.

Similarly, poor decision-making at work can arise when you assume things about your colleagues or superiors without checking your assumptions against reality. If you believe that your boss is unhappy with your performance, you might start acting defensively or withdrawing from important projects, even if there's no real evidence to support that belief. In the absence of receipts—such as a direct conversation with your boss or a performance review—you're operating on a false assumption that could undermine your professional growth.

On a larger scale, organizations that operate without receipts often fall prey to groupthink and poor strategic decisions. When leaders rely on gut feelings, assumptions, or the status quo rather than data, research, and thorough analysis, the company can head down a path of inefficiency, lost revenue, and missed opportunities. Whether you're an employee or a leader, living without receipts at work can limit your potential, damage your professional relationships, and hinder your long-term success.

Mental Health: Anxiety, Depression & Low Self-Esteem

When your thoughts aren't grounded in evidence, it's easy to slip into patterns of anxiety, negativity, and distorted self-perception. The brain craves certainty, and when it doesn't have it, it often fills in the gaps with worst-case scenarios and negative assumptions.

For people who struggle with anxiety, living without receipts often manifests as a constant state of worry. You might find yourself ruminating on potential outcomes that have little basis in reality, but because you haven't gathered the receipts to challenge those thoughts, they start to feel real. Consider this scenario: you begin to worry that a loved one is angry with you because they seemed quiet during dinner, even though there's no concrete evidence to support that worry. Over time, these unverified thoughts can create a chronic sense of unease and lead to heightened levels of anxiety.

Depression can also be fueled by living without receipts. When your thoughts are dominated by assumptions about failure, inadequacy, or hopelessness, it's easy to get trapped in a downward spiral. Without evidence to counteract these thoughts, they become ingrained, leading to feelings of worthlessness and despair. Someone experiencing depression might believe, *"I'm a failure"* or *"Nothing ever works out for me"*, even when there's plenty of evidence to suggest otherwise. Living without receipts reinforces these negative beliefs, making it harder to break free from the cycle of depression.

Low self-esteem is another byproduct of living without receipts. When your self-worth is based on assumptions or external validation rather than on a solid foundation of evidence, you're more likely to feel insecure or inadequate. Take the case of someone who believes their worth is tied to how others perceive them. Without receipts to verify those perceptions, they'll constantly seek approval and fear rejection. This leaves them vulnerable to the ups and downs of external validation rather than cultivating a stable sense of self grounded in their own achievements, values, and strengths.

Physical Health: The Stress Response

The connection between mind and body is well-established. When your thoughts are driven by assumptions, anxiety, or fear, your body responds accordingly. This is known as the stress response, and it's triggered when the brain perceives a threat—whether real or imagined.

When living without receipts, the brain often treats uncertainty as a threat, triggering the release of stress hormones like cortisol and adrenaline. These hormones prepare the body for the "fight or flight" response mentioned earlier, a survival mechanism that's useful in the face of actual danger but harmful when triggered by everyday worries and assumptions.

Chronic activation of the stress response can lead to a range of physical health problems, including headaches, muscle tension, digestive issues, and weakened immune function. Over time, prolonged stress can contribute to more serious conditions, such as heart disease, high blood pressure, and chronic pain.

If you're constantly worried about losing your job—despite having no concrete evidence to suggest that it's in jeopardy—your body remains in a heightened state of stress. This ongoing anxiety can disrupt your sleep, affect your ability to concentrate, and weaken your immune system, making you more susceptible to illness. Living without receipts in this context means that you're subjecting your body to unnecessary turmoil, simply because your mind is operating on assumptions rather than evidence.

The Psychological & Emotional Toll of Living Without Receipts

While the practical consequences of living without receipts are significant, the psychological and emotional toll is perhaps even more profound. When your mind is constantly operating on assumptions, half-truths, and unverified beliefs, it creates a mental environment characterized by uncertainty, fear, and lack of confidence.

Insecurity & Self-Doubt

One of the most immediate psychological effects of living without receipts is a pervasive sense of inadequacy and negative self-perception. When you don't have clear, objective evidence to support your beliefs or decisions, it's easy to feel unsure of yourself. You start to question your choices, second-guess your actions, and doubt your abilities.

Imagine you're leading a project at work but you're not sure if your team supports your vision. Without receipts—such as direct feedback or a clear understanding of your team's expectations—you might start to feel insecure about your leadership. You might question whether your ideas are good enough or whether your colleagues respect you. This insecurity can undermine your confidence and make it harder to lead effectively.

In personal relationships, insecurity often stems from a lack of receipts about the other person's feelings or intentions. If you're unsure whether your partner loves you or whether your friend values your friendship, you might start to feel anxious and insecure. Without clear communication (your receipts), you're left to interpret their actions based on your own fears and assumptions. This can lead to feelings of inadequacy as you start to believe that you're not worthy of love or friendship.

Insecurity is exhausting, creating a constant need for reassurance or validation. Living without receipts means that you're never fully certain of where you stand, which can lead to chronic feelings of self-doubt and a lack of confidence in both personal and professional settings.

Fear of Failure

Another psychological consequence of living without receipts is a heightened fear of failure. When your beliefs and decisions aren't grounded in evidence, failure feels more threatening because you don't have the tools to accurately assess the situation. Without receipts, every setback or challenge can feel like a catastrophic failure rather than a normal part of the learning and growth process.

Take the scenario of being asked to give a presentation at work. If you don't have receipts—such as past experience, positive feedback, or thorough preparation—you might start to feel paralyzed by the fear of failure. Without evidence to reassure you that you're capable, the thought of making a mistake or being judged by your colleagues becomes overwhelming.

This fear of failure can prevent you from taking risks or pursuing new opportunities. When you're constantly worried about failing, you're less likely to step outside your comfort zone or try something new. This limits your personal and professional growth, as you're stuck in a cycle of playing it safe and avoiding anything that might lead to failure.

However, when you have receipts to back up your decisions, the fear of failure becomes more manageable. You're able to approach challenges with a greater sense of confidence, knowing that you have the tools and resources to handle whatever comes your way.

Perfectionism

This is another emotional byproduct of living without receipts. When you don't have clear evidence to support your beliefs or decisions, you might feel the need to overcompensate by striving for perfection. This is often driven by a fear of making mistakes or being judged by others, and it can lead to an unhealthy obsession with getting everything "just right."

Perfectionism is exhausting because it's unattainable. No matter how hard you try, you'll never be able to achieve perfect results in every situation. However, when you're living without receipts, the pressure to be perfect can feel overwhelming. Without evidence to reassure you that "good enough" is truly good enough, you might push yourself to unrealistic standards, leading to burnout and dissatisfaction.

If you're working on a project at work and you don't have receipts in the form of clear expectations or feedback from your boss, you might find yourself obsessing over every detail. You might spend hours revising the project, second-guessing your choices, and worrying that it's not perfect. This not only drains your time and energy but also increases your stress and anxiety.

Living with receipts helps to counteract perfectionism by providing clarity and perspective. When you have concrete evidence that your work meets expectations, you're able to let go of the need for perfection and focus on doing your best. Receipts give you the confidence to trust your abilities and accept that mistakes are a natural part of growth.

Imposter Syndrome

This term refers to a phenomenon in which individuals feel like they're not as competent or capable as others perceive them to be. It's the feeling of being a fraud, even when there's evidence to suggest that you're doing well. Living without receipts can exacerbate imposter syndrome because it leaves you vulnerable to doubts and insecurities that aren't based in reality.

Picture someone who's recently been promoted to a leadership role but feels undeserving of it. In the absence of receipts—such as performance reviews, feedback from colleagues, or a clear understanding of why they were chosen—they might begin to believe they're unqualified or that the promotion was a mistake. This belief can spiral into feelings of inadequacy, self-doubt, and anxiety.

Imposter syndrome thrives in the absence of receipts. When you don't have concrete evidence to support your achievements, it's easy to discount your successes and focus on your perceived shortcomings. By gathering receipts, you can challenge imposter-driven thoughts and build a more accurate, grounded sense of self-worth.

The Impact of Living Without Receipts on Decision-Making

In addition to the psychological and emotional toll, living without receipts also has a significant impact on your decision-making abilities. When your decisions aren't based on evidence, they're more likely to be influenced by cognitive biases, emotions, and assumptions, leading to poor outcomes.

Decision Paralysis

One of the most common effects of living without receipts is decision paralysis—the inability to make a decision because you don't have enough information or confidence to move forward. When you're unsure of the facts or operating on assumptions, every option can feel overwhelming, and the fear of making the wrong choice can prevent you from making any choice at all.

Imagine you're trying to decide whether to accept a new job offer. Without receipts—such as a clear understanding of the job's benefits, salary, and long-term prospects—you might find yourself stuck in a state of indecision. You might worry about making the wrong choice, second-guess your instincts, or feel paralyzed by the uncertainty of the situation.

Decision paralysis is frustrating because it keeps you stuck in limbo. You're unable to move forward, and the longer you stay in that state, the more anxious and uncertain you feel. When you have receipts—like feedback from others in the industry or a clear sense of your priorities—you can make a more informed, confident choice.

Impulsive Decisions

While some people struggle with decision paralysis, others respond to uncertainty by making *impulsive* decisions. When you're living without receipts, it's tempting to make quick choices based on emotions or assumptions rather than taking the time to gather evidence and weigh your options.

For instance, if you're feeling stressed about a project at work, you might impulsively decide to quit your job, even though you haven't thoroughly considered the consequences. Or if you're feeling insecure in a relationship, you might decide to break up with your partner without having a clear conversation about your concerns.

Impulsive decisions can lead to regret because they're often based on temporary emotions rather than long-term considerations. Without receipts to guide your choices, you're more likely to act on impulse and make decisions that don't align with your values or goals.

Gathering receipts helps to counteract impulsive decision-making by giving you the tools to make thoughtful, informed choices. Taking time to gather evidence, reflect, and seek feedback helps you make decisions that align with your long-term well-being.

Breaking Free from the Cost of Living Without Receipts

While living without receipts can have serious consequences, the good news is you can break free from this pattern and develop an evidence-based mindset. The key is to become more intentional about gathering receipts and using them to guide your thoughts, decisions, and beliefs.

48

Developing a Receipt-Based Mindset

Building a receipt-based mindset begins with awareness. A mindset based on objective evidence prioritizes clarity and impartiality over assumptions, emotions, and biases. This doesn't mean dismissing your feelings or ignoring your intuition—it means balancing emotional responses with concrete, verifiable information.

Before reacting or deciding, pause to ask: *"What evidence supports this belief? Am I relying on assumptions, or on facts?"* Our perspective can be too limited or biased to see the full picture, so seeking feedback helps reveal blind spots and challenge unnoticed assumptions. Once you've identified a belief, test it against reality to see if it holds up. Being open to change means accepting that your first perspective might not be the right one. And consistently gathering and evaluating receipts makes the habit second nature.

By weaving these habits into daily life, you shift your focus from assumption to evidence and from uncertainty to clarity.

Seeking Feedback & Clarification

One of the most effective ways to gather receipts is to seek insight and clarity from others. Whether it's in a professional setting, a personal relationship, or a decision about your own life, feedback provides valuable information that can help you see the situation more clearly.

If you're feeling insecure about your performance at work, ask your boss for feedback. If you're unsure about the status of a relationship, have a direct conversation with the other person. By seeking clarification, you can replace your assumptions with actual receipts, which will help you make more informed decisions and feel more confident in your choices.

Reflecting on Past Experiences

Another way to gather receipts is to reflect on your past experiences and achievements. When you're feeling uncertain or doubting yourself, take the time to review the evidence of your past successes, challenges you've overcome, and the skills you've developed along the way.

Let's say, you're feeling anxious about a new professional role, remind yourself of the strides you've made in your current position. Reflect on the strategies you used, the feedback you received, and the lessons you learned. By gathering receipts from your own experiences, you can build a stronger sense of confidence and trust in your abilities.

Challenging Cognitive Biases

Cognitive biases like confirmation bias, catastrophizing, and black-and-white thinking can distort your perception of reality and lead to poor decision-making. To break free from these biases, it's important to actively challenge them by seeking out receipts that offer a more balanced perspective.

If you're catastrophizing about a potential outcome, ask yourself, *"What evidence do I have that this worst-case scenario is likely to happen?"* Similarly, if you're engaging in black-and-white thinking, ask yourself, *"Is there a middle ground here that I'm not considering?"* By challenging your cognitive biases and gathering receipts, you can start to see the situation more clearly and make decisions based on a fuller picture of reality.

Taking Action

Finally, breaking free from the cost of living without receipts requires taking action. It's not enough to gather receipts—you also need to use them to guide your decisions and choices. This means stepping outside your comfort zone, taking risks, and making decisions based on evidence, even when it feels uncomfortable or uncertain.

Here's how it looks in action: if you've gathered receipts that suggest you're ready for a new career opportunity, take the leap and apply for the job. If you've gathered receipts that suggest a relationship is no longer serving you, take action to address the issue or move on. By taking action based on receipts, you'll build momentum and create positive changes in your life.

The Rewards of Living with Receipts

Living without receipts comes with significant costs, but the rewards of living *with* receipts are equally profound. When your thoughts, decisions, and beliefs are grounded in evidence, you experience greater clarity, confidence, and peace of mind. You're able to navigate challenges with a sense of certainty, make decisions that align with your values, and cultivate healthier relationships with yourself and others.

The process of gathering receipts takes time and effort, but the benefits are well worth it. By developing a receipt-based mindset, you'll free yourself from the uncertainty, anxiety, and self-doubt that comes with living without evidence. You'll create a foundation of clarity and confidence that allows you to live a life grounded in truth, not assumptions.

As you continue to build your receipt-based mindset, remember that this is a lifelong practice. There'll be times when you slip back into old patterns of thinking, but by staying committed to gathering receipts and challenging your assumptions, you'll create a mental environment that supports growth, resilience, and well-being.

To deepen your understanding of how assumptions shape your reality, take a moment to look backward. We often don't realize how many of our past decisions were made without verified evidence until we're forced to face the consequences. This reflective exercise will help you identify moments when assumptions took the lead—and imagine how things might have turned out differently if receipts had guided you instead.

Exercise: Mindful Journaling Worksheet

- **Purpose**: To reflect on times when assumptions led to negative consequences.
- **Activity**: Journal about a time when you operated on an assumption that later turned out to be false. Your prompts can include:
  - *What assumption did I make, and how did it affect my actions?*
  - *What was the outcome, and how did I feel afterward?*
  - *If I'd gathered receipts beforehand, what might have changed?*

By confronting these moments honestly, you'll begin to build self-awareness around the hidden costs of assumption-driven thinking. More importantly, you'll sharpen your ability to pause before accepting a belief as truth—giving yourself the chance to verify rather than assume. Each reflection strengthens your internal accountability and helps you step closer to a life rooted in clarity.

The more you train your mind to question, pause, and validate, the more empowered you become. Living with a receipt-based mindset doesn't eliminate mistakes—it gives you the tools to correct course when they happen. It's about anchoring your choices in truth, not fear or fantasy.

But what happens when we become so convinced by our own thoughts that we don't even realize we're operating without receipts? When the story we tell ourselves feels so true that we stop questioning it altogether?

In the next chapter, we'll explore the subtle, slippery path of self-deception—how it begins, how it hides, and how to spot it before it takes root. Because even the smartest minds can fall for their own stories when facts aren't part of the narrative.

Chapter 5: The Road to Self-Deception

This chapter breaks down how easily we deceive ourselves when we don't validate our thoughts. It illustrates the subtle ways in which the brain tricks us into believing falsehoods, and how this can lead to long-term problems.

Self-deception is one of the most subtle yet destructive forces in human behavior. It's the process of convincing ourselves of something that isn't true—fooling not only others, but also ourselves. Unlike deliberate dishonesty, self-deception often happens unconsciously, making it difficult to recognize and even harder to break free from. We can believe we're acting in our best interests, telling ourselves stories that fit our desires, fears, and biases, all while constructing a version of reality that is dangerously disconnected from the truth.

This chapter examines how we unconsciously delude ourselves, why it happens, and how it affects various aspects of our lives. We'll explore the cognitive mechanisms that lead to self-deception, the role of emotional needs in distorting our perception, and the long-term consequences of living with a distorted sense of reality. Most importantly, we'll discuss practical steps to spot when you're heading toward self-deception—and how to steer back to objective truth, armed with your receipts to ensure your beliefs align with reality.

What Is Self-Deception?

Before exploring the mechanics, it's important to understand what self-deception is—and how it differs from intentional deception. When we think of deception, we often think of people deliberately lying or manipulating the truth to gain some advantage or avoid responsibility. But self-deception is different—it's the act of lying to ourselves, convincing oneself of things that aren't true, and *truly believing* those lies. It's not about manipulating others; it's about manipulating our own perception of reality.

Self-deception can take many forms, from small, everyday distortions of the truth to larger, life-altering delusions. You might convince yourself that your relationship is healthy when deep down, you know it's not. You might tell yourself that your work performance is stellar, even though you've been avoiding challenging tasks. Or you might believe that you're fine mentally and emotionally, even as signs of burnout, anxiety, or depression begin to emerge. Self-deception isn't just about avoiding uncomfortable truths—it's also about building an entire narrative that makes those truths seem irrelevant or invisible.

At the core of self-deception is a refusal to confront reality. It's easier to ignore or distort difficult facts than it is to face them head-on. We tell ourselves stories to justify our actions, our relationships, and our decisions, creating a version of reality that makes us feel safe, comfortable, and in control. But over time, self-deception can lead us down a dangerous path, where the gap between what we believe and what's actually true becomes so wide that it starts to harm our mental health, relationships, and personal growth.

The Cognitive Mechanics of Self-Deception

To understand how self-deception happens, we need to take a closer look at the *cognitive mechanisms* that make it possible. Self-deception doesn't happen overnight—it's a gradual process that involves several cognitive biases and mental shortcuts. These mental processes are designed to make our thinking more efficient, but they can also lead us down the road to self-deception.

Confirmation Bias

This is one of the most well-known cognitive biases, and it plays a central role in self-deception. As mentioned in previous chapters, it's the tendency to seek out information that confirms what we already believe while ignoring or dismissing information that contradicts those beliefs. In the context of self-deception, confirmation bias allows us to build a selective version of reality that aligns with our desires, fears, or preconceived notions.

If you see yourself as a hard-working employee, you might recall the times you stayed late or tackled difficult tasks. But you might conveniently forget the days when you procrastinated or didn't meet deadlines. Over time, confirmation bias reinforces your belief that you're a diligent worker, even if the reality is more complicated.

Confirmation bias allows us to maintain a consistent self-image, even when that image doesn't match reality. It gives us a sense of control and certainty, but at the cost of ignoring inconvenient truths that could help us grow and improve.

Cognitive Dissonance

This is another key mechanism that fuels self-deception. *Cognitive dissonance* occurs when we hold two conflicting beliefs, or when our actions contradict our beliefs. This creates a feeling of discomfort, and to reduce this discomfort, we often engage in self-deception.

For instance, let's say you believe that you're an honest person, but you find yourself telling a small lie to avoid confrontation. This creates cognitive dissonance because your action (lying) conflicts with your belief (that you're honest). To reduce this dissonance, you might deceive yourself by justifying the lie: "*It wasn't a big deal, I didn't want to hurt their feelings"*, or *"Everyone lies sometimes"*. These rationalizations allow you to maintain your self-image as an honest person, even though your actions contradict that belief.

Cognitive dissonance can lead to self-deception because it encourages us to find ways to reconcile our actions with our beliefs, even if that means distorting the truth. Instead of acknowledging that we've acted in ways that don't align with our values, we change our perception of the situation to avoid the discomfort of dissonance.

The Self-Serving Bias

This bias is defined as the tendency to attribute positive outcomes to our own abilities and efforts, while attributing negative outcomes to external factors. It helps protect our self-esteem but also plays a major role in self-deception. When things go well, we take credit for our success. When things go wrong, we blame circumstances beyond our control.

If you excel on a project at work, you might attribute it to your talent and effort. But if the project doesn't go as planned, you might blame external factors like an uncooperative team, unclear instructions, or bad timing. The *self-serving bias* allows us to maintain a positive self-image, but it also prevents us from taking responsibility for our mistakes or shortcomings.

Over time, this can lead to self-deception because it encourages us to view ourselves in an overly positive light. We begin to believe that we're more competent, capable, or virtuous than we actually are, and we ignore the feedback or evidence that suggests otherwise.

The Emotional Drivers of Self-Deception

While cognitive biases play a significant role in self-deception, *emotions* are often the driving force behind why we deceive ourselves. At its core, self-deception is about avoiding emotional discomfort. We deceive ourselves because we don't want to face painful truths, experience failure, or feel vulnerable. Our emotional needs—such as the need for security, approval, or control—often lead us to construct false narratives that protect us from these difficult emotions.

The Need for Security

Security is one of the most common emotional drivers of self-deception. As human beings, we crave security, certainty, and stability. We want to believe that our lives are on the right track, that we're making the right decisions, and that we're in control of our circumstances. When our sense of security is threatened—whether by a relationship issue, a career setback, or a personal failure—we often deceive ourselves to avoid facing the reality of uncertainty.

If you're in a relationship that's no longer fulfilling, you might deceive yourself into believing that things are fine because the alternative—acknowledging that the relationship is in trouble—feels too destabilizing. You might ignore the red flags, downplay your own feelings of dissatisfaction, or convince yourself that things will get better on their own. In doing so, you create a false sense of security, even though the reality of the situation remains unresolved.

This need for security can keep us trapped in self-deception for long periods of time. We convince ourselves that everything is fine, even when the evidence suggests otherwise, because the truth feels too uncertain or threatening to confront.

The Desire for Approval

Another powerful emotional driver of self-deception is the need for validation. Wanting to be liked, accepted, and valued can lead us to deceive ourselves about who we are or how we're perceived. We might tell ourselves that we're more successful, attractive, or likable than we really are because the alternative—facing the possibility that others don't see us in the way we want to be seen—feels too painful.

Imagine believing that your friends admire and respect you, even when there are signs they might not. You might overlook subtle cues of disinterest, steer clear of difficult conversations, or explain away dismissive behavior as just a temporary mood. This kind of self-deception helps preserve the belief that you're well-liked, but it also keeps you from confronting the reality of your relationships.

The desire for approval can also lead to self-deception in the workplace. You might convince yourself that your boss is happy with your performance, even if you've received critical feedback, because the thought of not meeting expectations feels too threatening to your self-esteem. In doing so, you create a version of reality that protects your ego, but it also prevents you from making the changes necessary to improve your performance.

The Fear of Vulnerability

Self-deception is often driven by an aversion to making ourselves vulnerable. Vulnerability means acknowledging our weaknesses, fears, and imperfections, and this can be incredibly uncomfortable. Rather than face the reality of our vulnerabilities, we deceive ourselves into believing that we're stronger, more capable, or more confident than we actually are.

There are times, you might tell yourself that you don't need help or support, even when you're struggling, because asking for help would make you feel vulnerable. You might convince yourself that you can handle everything on your own, even if the evidence suggests otherwise. This self-deception allows you to maintain the illusion of strength, but it also isolates you from the support and connection that you need.

The fear of vulnerability can also manifest in relationships. You might deceive yourself into believing that you don't need emotional intimacy or that you're fine with surface-level connections because the thought of opening up and being vulnerable feels too risky. This self-deception shields you from the discomfort of vulnerability but also blocks deeper, more meaningful connections.

The Consequences of Self-Deception

While self-deception might provide temporary relief from emotional discomfort, the long-term consequences can be significant. Living with a distorted sense of reality can affect every aspect of your life, from your mental health and relationships to your career and personal growth.

Mental & Emotional Exhaustion

Maintaining a false version of reality demands significant mental energy. You have to constantly justify your actions, suppress uncomfortable truths, and construct narratives that fit your self-deception. Over time, these mental gymnastics can lead to exhaustion as your mind becomes overwhelmed by the effort to keep up the façade.

If you're deceiving yourself about the state of your relationship, you might spend a lot of time and energy convincing yourself that everything is fine. You might rationalize your partner's behavior, avoid difficult conversations, and suppress your own feelings of dissatisfaction. This constant effort to maintain the deception can leave you feeling drained and emotionally depleted.

In addition to mental exhaustion, self-deception can also lead to emotional exhaustion. When you're constantly avoiding uncomfortable truths, you're also avoiding the emotions that come with them. This emotional avoidance can create a sense of numbness or disconnection as you become increasingly detached from your own feelings.

Stunted Personal Growth

Self-deception about your abilities, relationships, or circumstances blinds you to the areas where you need to grow. Instead of confronting your weaknesses or addressing your challenges, you create a version of reality that allows you to stay in your comfort zone.

If you deceive yourself into believing that you're already a great leader, you might avoid seeking feedback or developing new skills. You might ignore the areas where you need to improve, which prevents you from reaching your full potential. Similarly, if you deceive yourself about the state of your health, you might avoid making necessary lifestyle changes, which can have long-term consequences for your well-being.

Self-deception keeps you stuck in a state of complacency. It allows you to maintain the status quo, but it also prevents you from achieving the growth and progress that come from confronting challenges and embracing change.

Damaged Relationships

When you deceive yourself about your own behavior, feelings, or needs, it's difficult to have honest, authentic connections with others. You might find yourself avoiding difficult conversations, suppressing your true feelings, or projecting your insecurities onto your relationships.

Suppose that you deceive yourself into believing that you don't need emotional intimacy, you might keep your partner at a distance, which can create a sense of emotional disconnection. Or if you deceive yourself into believing that your friend group is supportive and drama-free, you might ignore the toxic dynamics that are causing tension. Over time, these deceptions can erode trust, communication, and intimacy in your relationships.

In addition to damaging your relationships with others, self-deception can also damage your relationship with yourself. When you're constantly lying to yourself, you lose touch with your own needs, values, and emotions. This can create a sense of inner conflict, as your true self is at odds with the version of reality you've constructed.

Missed Opportunities

When you deceive yourself about your abilities or circumstances, you're less likely to take risks or pursue new opportunities. You might convince yourself that you're not ready for a promotion, that you don't have what it takes to start your own business, or that you're not capable of pursuing a new passion. This self-deception keeps you playing small, even when there's evidence to suggest that you're capable of more.

If you deceive yourself into believing that you're not creative, you might avoid pursuing artistic or innovative projects, even though you have the potential to excel in those areas. Or if you deceive yourself into believing that you're not very good at public speaking, you might turn down opportunities to give presentations or lead workshops, even though those opportunities could help you grow professionally.

Self-deception limits your ability to take advantage of opportunities for growth, learning, and success. It keeps you stuck in a narrative of limitations, even when the reality is that you're capable of more than you realize.

Breaking Free from Self-Deception

While the road to self-deception is a slippery slope, you can break free and build a more honest, grounded relationship with yourself and the world around you. The key is to become more aware of your cognitive biases, emotional needs, and the ways in which you deceive yourself. By gathering receipts and using them to challenge your self-deception, you can begin to see reality more clearly and make choices that are aligned with the truth.

Cultivating Self-Awareness

This is the first step in breaking free from self-deception. Cultivating self-awareness means becoming more attuned to your thoughts, emotions, and behaviors, and recognizing when you're engaging in self-deception. Self-awareness allows you to identify the areas where you're avoiding uncomfortable truths or distorting reality to fit your desires or fears.

One way to cultivate self-awareness is through mindfulness practices, such as meditation or journaling. These practices can help you become more present with your thoughts and emotions, allowing you to observe them without judgment. By developing a greater sense of self-awareness, you can start to recognize when you're slipping into self-deception and take steps to address it.

Challenging Your Cognitive Biases

As we've examined previously, cognitive biases like confirmation bias, cognitive dissonance, and the self-serving bias play a major role in self-deception. To break free from these biases, it's important to actively challenge them by seeking out receipts that provide a more balanced perspective.

If you're prone to confirmation bias, make a conscious effort to seek out information that challenges your beliefs. If you tend to justify your actions through cognitive dissonance, practice taking responsibility for your mistakes rather than rationalizing them. By challenging your cognitive biases, you can develop a more objective view of reality and reduce the likelihood of self-deception.

Embracing Vulnerability

Vulnerability can be scary, but it's also essential for growth and authenticity. Embracing it means being willing to confront uncomfortable truths, acknowledge your weaknesses, and admit when you're wrong.

Let's say, you've been deceiving yourself about the state of your relationship, embracing vulnerability might mean having a difficult conversation with your partner about your feelings. If you've been deceiving yourself about your abilities, embracing vulnerability might mean seeking feedback or admitting that you need help.

By embracing vulnerability, you open yourself up to the possibility of growth, connection, and transformation. You allow yourself to be seen for who you truly are rather than hiding behind a façade of self-deception.

Seeking Feedback

Because blind spots are hard to see on our own, feedback from trusted friends, colleagues, or mentors can reveal where self-deception may be at work.

If you've been deceiving yourself about your performance at work, asking for feedback from your boss or coworkers can provide you with objective information about your strengths and areas for improvement. If you've been deceiving yourself about the health of your personal relationships, seeking feedback from trusted friends can help you gain clarity.

By seeking feedback, you gather receipts that challenge your self-deception and provide you with a more accurate view of reality.

Taking Accountability

Finally, breaking free from self-deception requires holding yourself accountable for your actions and decisions. This means acknowledging when you've been wrong, taking responsibility for your mistakes, and making a commitment to live in alignment with the truth.

Taking accountability doesn't mean being overly critical of yourself or dwelling on past mistakes. Instead, it means being honest with yourself about where you've gone wrong and taking proactive steps to make things right. It means owning your choices, learning from your experiences, and committing to living a life that's grounded in reality, not self-deception.

Living with Honesty & Integrity

The road to self-deception is easy to travel, but it's also possible to turn around and find your way back to the truth. By becoming more aware of your cognitive biases, emotional needs, and the ways in which you deceive yourself, you can start to break free from the patterns of self-deception and live a life that's rooted in sincerity and authenticity.

Living with honesty and integrity means facing uncomfortable truths, embracing vulnerability, and taking responsibility for your actions. It means gathering receipts and using them to guide your decisions and beliefs. While the process of breaking free from self-deception can be challenging, the rewards are well worth the effort.

When you live with honesty and integrity, you create a foundation of trust, clarity, and authenticity in your relationships, your career, and your personal growth. You free yourself from the mental and emotional exhaustion of maintaining a false version of reality, and you open yourself up to the possibility of growth, connection, and fulfillment.

As you continue on your journey toward a receipt-based mindset, remember that the road to self-deception is one that we all travel at times. What matters isn't that you never deceive yourself but that you have the tools and awareness to recognize when it's happening and take steps to course correct. By living with honesty and integrity, you create a life that's aligned with the truth, and you set yourself on a path toward greater authenticity, fulfillment, and personal growth.

As we've seen, self-deception thrives when we don't challenge our thoughts with clear, objective evidence. In the next chapter, we'll explore practical, actionable ways to start gathering those receipts—so you can ground your decisions in truth and guard against the mental traps we've uncovered here.

Chapter 6: How to Find Your Receipts

One of the most powerful tools you can develop is the ability to ask good questions. The quality of your questions directly shapes the quality of your answers, guiding you toward deeper understanding and clarity.

This chapter will equip you with practical skills to uncover truth by asking the right questions, identifying reliable evidence, and overcoming mental shortcuts that cloud judgment. You'll explore how to foster curiosity, break down assumptions, and strengthen emotional intelligence through effective questioning. To bring these strategies to life, we'll follow four relatable characters—Rhonda, Sara, Ronald, and Carmen— each navigating unique struggles with self-deception, fear, and unverified beliefs. Their stories will show how these tools apply to real-world challenges and how learning to seek receipts can transform your thinking and your life.

Developing the Skill of Asking the Right Questions

We've established that asking the right questions is essential for uncovering truth and living grounded in facts. But how do you make this skill a natural part of your thinking? It requires practice, reflection, and sometimes humility. Asking strong questions means framing them clearly and specifically—and being willing to face answers you might not want to hear.

In the journey to cultivate this skill, it's crucial to recognize that asking the right questions goes beyond surface-level inquiries. It requires a deep dive into your assumptions, emotional triggers, and cognitive biases. It means developing a mindset that values truth and clarity over comfort and ego preservation. In this extended chapter, we'll explore practical techniques, common challenges, and mental frameworks that can help you become more adept at asking the right questions, whether in your personal life, professional settings, or even within your internal dialogue.

The Foundation of Curiosity: Cultivating a Curious Mindset

At the heart of asking the right questions is curiosity. A curious mindset is essential because it drives us to seek answers and look beyond what's immediately visible. Curiosity transforms mundane questions into powerful inquiries that can reveal hidden truths. However, many people struggle with curiosity, especially when the answers may lead them into uncomfortable or unfamiliar territory.

To develop curiosity, you need to start viewing every situation as an opportunity to learn. Instead of approaching life with the assumption that you already know all the answers, embrace the idea that there's always more to uncover. This doesn't mean second-guessing yourself at every turn—it means approaching each situation with an open mind, ready to explore different possibilities and perspectives.

The following are some strategies to foster curiosity:

- **Ask "Why" More Often:** Challenge yourself to ask "why" multiple times in a row when faced with a situation. If you're feeling frustrated at work, ask yourself, *"Why am I frustrated?"* Your first answer might be, *"Because my boss doesn't listen."* Then ask, *"Why do I feel my boss doesn't listen?"* This will lead you deeper into the issue, helping you identify the root cause rather than staying stuck in surface-level frustration.
- **Explore Different Perspectives:** Get into the habit of seeing things from different viewpoints. When you ask a question, consider how someone else might approach the same issue. How would a child, a colleague, or someone from a different cultural background see this situation? This

helps broaden your perspective and leads to more nuanced questions.

- **Embrace Not Knowing:** Curiosity flourishes when we embrace uncertainty and the unknown. Often, we shy away from asking certain questions because we're afraid of not having the answers or we fear looking incompetent. However, admitting that you don't know something is the first step toward growth. Instead of avoiding difficult topics, lean into them with curiosity and a willingness to learn.

Moving from Assumptions to Inquiries: Breaking Mental Shortcuts

Our brains are wired to make quick decisions based on assumptions and mental shortcuts. While these shortcuts are useful in many situations, they can also lead us to false conclusions. One of the biggest barriers to asking the right questions is the assumption that we already know the answer, which causes us to ask biased questions that reaffirm what we believe instead of revealing the truth.

To ask better questions, it's important to challenge assumptions. Start by recognizing when you're assuming something, especially when it's based on incomplete information or emotions. If you think a coworker is upset with you because they haven't replied to your message, pause and ask yourself, *"What am I assuming here?"* By breaking down your assumptions, you can create more open-ended questions.

Some practical techniques for overcoming assumptions include:

- **Reframing Your Questions:** Instead of asking questions that reinforce your assumptions—such as *"Why are you ignoring me?"*—try asking more open questions like, *"Is everything okay? I haven't heard from you and wanted to check in."*

The goal is to create space for new information rather than confirming your fears or biases.

- **Adopting a Beginner's Mind:** This concept comes from Zen Buddhism and involves approaching every situation as if you're encountering it for the first time. Even if you've dealt with similar situations before, don't assume that you already know the answers. By adopting a beginner's mind, you free yourself from assumptions and open up to the possibility of learning something new.

- **Checking Your Emotional Temperature:** When emotions run high, we tend to make more assumptions. Before asking a question, take a moment to assess your emotional state. Are you angry, anxious, or defensive? If so, you might be asking questions out of a need to justify your feelings rather than seek clarity. Calm yourself before proceeding with your inquiry.

Crafting Clear & Specific Questions

One of the most common mistakes people make when asking questions is being too vague or general. A vague question is unlikely to elicit a clear answer, and it often leads to confusion, frustration, or incomplete responses. To develop the skill of asking the right questions, it's essential to practice being clear and specific.

The more precise your question, the better the quality of the answer you're likely to receive. Instead of asking, *"Why did the project fail?"* a more specific question might be, *"What specific challenges did we face in meeting the project deadlines, and how can we address them moving forward?"*

Clear and specific questions do the following:

- **Eliminate Ambiguity:** They remove any guesswork and allow the person answering to focus on what's relevant.

When your questions are clear, the answers are more likely to be accurate and actionable.

- **Encourage Focus:** Specific questions encourage the person (or yourself) to focus on the core issue rather than getting lost in tangential topics. This ensures that you're addressing the heart of the matter.

- **Increase Engagement:** In both personal and professional settings, people are more likely to engage in meaningful conversations when the questions are specific. A vague question like, *"How's everything going?"* might elicit a one-word answer, while a more focused question like, *"What challenges are you currently facing in your role?"* invites a deeper response.

Here's how to craft clear and specific questions:

- **Focus on Actionable Details:** Avoid abstract or broad questions like, *"What went wrong?"* Instead, ask, *"What specific steps led to this outcome, and what could be done differently next time?"* This ensures that the answer will provide you with actionable information you can use moving forward.

- **Avoid Overloading the Question:** Sometimes we try to pack too much into a single question, which can overwhelm the person answering. Keep your questions focused and straightforward, tackling one issue at a time. Instead of asking, *"Why did the project fail, and how can we fix it next time?"*, break it into two questions: *"What factors contributed to the failure?"* and *"What can we do differently next time?"*

- **Use the Funnel Technique:** Start with broader questions to gather general information and then follow up with more specific questions to drill down into the details. This approach ensures that you don't jump to conclusions too quickly, allowing you to explore the topic more thoroughly.

The Importance of Open-Ended Questions

The way a question is framed can limit the depth of the response. Closed-ended questions—those that can be answered with a simple "yes" or "no"—are often useful in gathering specific, factual information, but they rarely lead to deeper understanding. If your goal is to uncover insights, solve complex problems, or understand someone's perspective, open-ended questions are far more effective.

Open-ended questions invite reflection and dialogue. They encourage the person answering to share more details, explore their thoughts, and provide insights that might not have emerged otherwise. In contrast, closed-ended questions can shut down the conversation prematurely, leaving you with incomplete answers.

Below are some tips for using open-ended questions effectively:

- **Start with "How," "What," or "Why":** These naturally lead to more expansive answers. Instead of asking, *"Did you like the presentation?"*, try asking, *"What did you think of the presentation?"* This opens the door to a broader conversation and allows the person to share their full perspective.
- **Encourage Exploration:** Open-ended questions encourage people to explore their thoughts and feelings in more depth. Instead of asking, *"Did you enjoy the movie?"*, ask, *"How did the movie make you feel?"* This encourages reflection on their emotional experience and can lead to a more meaningful discussion.
- **Create a Safe Space for Dialogue:** When asking open questions, it's important to create an environment where the person feels comfortable sharing their thoughts. Avoid interrupting, judging, or leading them toward a specific answer. Let the conversation unfold naturally and be

prepared to follow up with additional questions based on their response.

Asking Questions with Emotional Intelligence

Asking the right questions isn't just about gathering information—it's also about fostering understanding and building stronger relationships. This is where *emotional intelligence* (EQ) plays a crucial role. Emotional intelligence refers to the ability to recognize, understand, and manage your own emotions and the emotions of others. When you combine emotional intelligence with the skill of asking questions, you create a powerful tool for effective communication and problem-solving.

To ask questions with emotional intelligence, consider the following:

- **Be Aware of Timing:** Timing is crucial when asking sensitive questions. If someone is upset, frustrated, or overwhelmed, they may not be in the right emotional space to answer thoughtfully. In these situations, it's important to recognize when to wait and when to proceed. Instead of confronting a colleague immediately after a heated meeting, wait until emotions have settled before asking for feedback.
- **Use Empathy:** This is the ability to understand and share another person's feelings. When asking questions, use empathy to guide your approach. If you need to address a sensitive issue with a friend, ask yourself how you'd feel in their shoes. This will help you frame your question in a way that's compassionate and non-threatening. An empathetic question might be, *"I've noticed you've been quieter than usual lately—is there anything on your mind that you'd like to talk about?"*
- **Pay Attention to Nonverbal Cues:** When you ask a question, pay attention to the other person's body language, tone of voice, and facial expressions. These nonverbal cues

can reveal how someone is feeling and whether they're comfortable with the conversation. If you sense discomfort, be prepared to adjust your approach or offer reassurance.

The Role of Reflection: Learning from Your Questions

Developing the skill of asking the right questions is an ongoing process that requires reflection. After a conversation or situation in which you've asked important questions, take some time to reflect on the outcome. Did the questions lead to the answers you were seeking? Did they foster deeper understanding or problem-solving? What could you have done differently?

By regularly reflecting on your questioning technique, you can identify areas for improvement and refine your approach over time. Keep a journal or make mental notes of the questions that worked well and those that didn't. Over time, this practice will help you become more adept at framing questions that lead to meaningful insights.

Here's how to integrate reflection into your question-asking practice:

- **Analyze the Responses:** After you've asked a question, take a closer look at the answer. Did the response provide clarity? Was it detailed and thoughtful, or was it vague and incomplete? If it didn't meet your expectations, consider how you could have phrased the question differently.
- **Reflect on the Conversation Dynamics:** Think about how the conversation flowed after you asked your question. Did it lead to a productive dialogue, or did it stall? Were there moments when the other person seemed hesitant or uncomfortable? Use this feedback to adjust your questioning style in future interactions.

- **Learn from Mistakes:** Asking the wrong question is part of learning. When you reflect on your mistakes, you can learn valuable lessons about what works and what doesn't. The key is to keep practicing and refining your technique.

Mastering the Art of Asking Questions

Asking the right questions is a powerful tool for uncovering truth, solving problems, and building strong relationships. It requires curiosity, clarity, emotional intelligence, and a willingness to challenge your own assumptions. By developing the skill of asking thoughtful, specific, and open-ended questions, you can create a foundation for deeper understanding and more meaningful conversations.

Incorporating these techniques into your daily life will help you navigate complex situations with greater ease, whether you're solving a professional challenge, addressing a personal issue, or seeking clarity within your own mind. The more you practice, the more natural this skill will become, allowing you to live a life grounded in truth and clarity.

Understanding the Purpose Behind Your Questions

Before diving into any inquiry, it's important to first ask yourself, *What is the purpose of my question?* In many situations, people tend to ask questions not to genuinely seek answers but rather to reinforce what they already believe. If you're angry at a partner, you might ask a question like, *"Why do you always ignore my needs?"* This question is loaded with assumptions and is emotionally charged. It's not intended to seek clarity or understanding—it's a question born out of frustration, intended to corner the other person into admitting fault.

The purpose behind your question should be rooted in one of these three reasons (or perhaps even all of them):

- to gain clarity
- to seek understanding
- to gather evidence

If you're not clear about why you're asking a question, you risk framing it in a way that leads to defensiveness or unproductive answers. When you approach a situation from a place of curiosity rather than accusation, you open the door to learning the truth rather than reinforcing your own biases.

Let's look at a different way to frame the same question from above. Instead of, *"Why do you always ignore my needs?"*, you could ask, *"I've been feeling unheard lately. Can we talk about how we can improve our communication to make sure both of our needs are met."* This version of the question is framed to encourage dialogue rather than defensiveness. It's aimed at finding solutions, not assigning blame.

Breaking Down Complex Questions

Some situations are complex, and a single question often won't capture the full scope of the problem. When this occurs, it's helpful to break down complex issues into smaller, manageable questions. This process is known as deconstructing a question, and it allows you to focus on different components of the problem one at a time.

If you're trying to understand why a project at work failed, you might feel overwhelmed by the complexity of the situation. Instead of asking a vague question like, *"Why did the project fail?"*, you could break it down into smaller, more specific questions:

- *"Were there any misunderstandings about the project's objectives from the beginning?"*
- *"Did we allocate enough resources to complete the project successfully?"*

- *"Were there any external factors that impacted the project's progress?"*

By breaking the issue into smaller questions, you can start to gather specific information that leads to a clearer understanding of the bigger picture. This approach not only helps you uncover more detailed evidence but also helps you focus on the root causes of the issue rather than get stuck in broad, overwhelming inquiries.

Learning to Embrace Silence

Sometimes, the best questions are followed by silence. This is particularly true in conversations in which emotions are involved, such as difficult discussions with loved ones, friends, or colleagues. After you've asked a question, resist the urge to fill the silence with more words. People often feel compelled to explain further or clarify their thoughts when given space to do so, and this can lead to valuable insights.

Silence also gives you time to reflect on the answers you receive. Rather than jumping to conclusions or reacting emotionally, pause and allow yourself to process the response. Silence is a powerful tool in effective communication, and when used wisely, can reveal much more than immediate reactions.

In a conflict resolution situation, after asking a question like, *"Can you help me understand why you reacted the way you did during our last conversation?",* giving the other person space to think will allow them to provide a more thoughtful, insightful response rather than reacting defensively.

Exploring Different Types of Evidence

Asking the right questions sets the stage for finding the right answers. But where do you *look* for those answers? In this section, we'll explore the various types of evidence that can help you build a clearer understanding of any situation. Evidence comes in many forms, and knowing which type to seek out can significantly improve your ability to make decisions based on facts.

Direct Evidence

This is the most straightforward type of evidence—it's based on firsthand experience or direct observation. This type of evidence includes things like personal testimonies, one-on-one conversations, or witnessing events yourself. Direct evidence is powerful because it leaves little room for interpretation—what you saw, heard, or experienced firsthand is generally considered reliable.

If you're questioning a friend's commitment to a project, direct evidence might include conversations you've had with them in which they expressed disinterest or a lack of enthusiasm. You could also point to specific instances when they failed to follow through on their responsibilities. These firsthand observations provide clear, direct evidence of their behavior.

Circumstantial Evidence

While not as strong as direct evidence, circumstantial evidence can still be useful in building a case or understanding a situation. It's based on inference rather than direct observation, and it relies on indirect signs or patterns to suggest that something is true. However, circumstantial evidence should be used with caution, as it can be easily misinterpreted.

Imagine you notice that your partner has been distant lately and spending more time at work—you might infer that they're avoiding you. While this could be true, it's also possible that they're dealing with stress at work or managing other responsibilities. Without direct evidence (such as a conversation about their feelings), you're relying on circumstantial evidence to draw your conclusions.

Historical Evidence

This type of evidence involves looking at past events, behaviors, or patterns to inform your understanding of the present. It can be particularly useful in relationships or professional settings where patterns of behavior often repeat themselves. By examining how someone has behaved in similar situations in the past, you can make more informed predictions about how they'll behave in the future.

If you've noticed that a colleague consistently misses deadlines when they're working on projects alone, you can use this historical evidence to anticipate future behavior. This doesn't mean that you should make unfair assumptions, but it allows you to plan for potential challenges based on past patterns.

Documentary Evidence

These are physical or digital records that provide verifiable proof. Examples include emails, contracts, written agreements, text messages, or financial statements. It's valuable because it's fairly concrete and often leaves little room for interpretation.

If you're disputing a charge on your credit card bill, having a receipt or record of the transaction would provide proof to support your claim. In professional settings, keeping records of communications or agreements can prevent misunderstandings and provide clear evidence if a conflict arises.

Testimonial Evidence

This form of evidence is based on the statements or accounts of others. It's often used in legal settings but can also be helpful in personal or professional situations. Testimonial evidence relies on someone else's perspective or expertise to provide insight into a situation. However, like circumstantial evidence, testimonial evidence should be weighed carefully, as it can be influenced by the person's biases or perceptions.

If you're trying to understand why a friend has been acting differently, you might ask another friend for their opinion or insight. While this can be helpful, remember that their view is subjective and should be cross-checked with other forms of evidence before drawing conclusions.

Avoiding Common Pitfalls in Evidence Gathering

Now that we've covered the different types of evidence, it's important to recognize common missteps that can occur when gathering it. Not all evidence is created equal, and just because you've collected some form of it doesn't mean that it's reliable. Below, we'll look at a few pitfalls to be mindful of when gathering evidence to support your beliefs or decisions.

Selective Attention

This is the tendency to focus on evidence that supports your existing beliefs while ignoring or downplaying evidence that contradicts them. Selective attention is a form of confirmation bias in which your mind unconsciously filters out information that doesn't fit your narrative.

Case in point, if you believe that a colleague is lazy, you might only pay attention to the times when they've missed deadlines or failed to contribute to team meetings. You might ignore the instances when they worked late or helped with tasks that weren't part of their responsibilities. To avoid selective attention, it's important to actively seek out evidence that challenges your assumptions.

Cherry-Picking Evidence

These are similar to selective attention but involve deliberately choosing pieces of evidence that support your argument while ignoring others that might weaken it. Cherry-picking evidence can happen in personal relationships, workplace disputes, or even when making decisions about your own life.

If you're arguing with your partner and trying to prove that they don't care about you, you might focus on the one time they forgot your birthday while conveniently ignoring all the other ways they've shown love and care. To avoid cherry-picking, make an effort to consider all the evidence, not just the parts that reinforce your point of view.

Emotional Reasoning

As mentioned in chapter 2, this pitfall occurs when you allow your feelings to dictate your perception of reality rather than relying on objective evidence. While emotions are important and valid, they're not always reliable indicators of the truth. Emotional reasoning can lead you to interpret events through a distorted lens, causing you to draw conclusions based on how you feel rather than what's actually happening.

In moments of relational insecurity, it's easy to interpret neutral actions from a partner as signs of disinterest or neglect. Instead of reacting to those emotions, take a step back and ask:" What *evidence supports this belief? Are there other ways to understand their behavior?"* By focusing on the facts rather than the feeling, you create space for a more balanced and grounded response.

Overgeneralization

This cognitive distortion, which was first introduced in chapter 3, is the tendency to take a single piece of evidence and apply it to a broader situation. Overgeneralization leads you to draw sweeping conclusions based on limited or isolated incidents. It often stems from a desire to make sense of complex situations by simplifying them but can result in faulty reasoning.

Consider this scenario: your partner forgets to do something nice for you once, overgeneralization might lead you to think: *"They never do anything thoughtful for me"*, even though this isn't true. To avoid overgeneralization, remind yourself that one isolated incident doesn't define the entire situation. Look for patterns and consistent behavior rather than focusing on single events.

Critical Thinking: Tools for Analyzing & Evaluating Evidence

Once you've gathered the necessary evidence, the next step is to analyze and evaluate it. This is where critical thinking becomes invaluable. It allows you to process information in a structured, logical way, ensuring your conclusions are based on sound reasoning rather than emotions or assumptions.

The following are some tools and strategies for evaluating evidence and making more informed decisions.

The Socratic Method

This disciplined questioning technique helps you explore the deeper meaning behind your beliefs and assumptions. By continuously asking "why" and "how," you can uncover the underlying logic (or lack thereof) in your thinking. The Socratic method encourages you to challenge your assumptions, consider alternative perspectives, and arrive at conclusions that are well-supported by evidence.

Suppose you're feeling frustrated with a friend and believe they're being selfish, you might start by asking yourself:

- *Why do I believe they're being selfish?*
- *What evidence do I have to support this belief?*
- *Is there another way to interpret their behavior?*
- *How does this belief align with their past actions?*

Through this process of questioning, you can evaluate the validity of your beliefs and ensure that they're grounded in reality rather than assumptions.

Evaluating the Credibility of Your Sources

Not all evidence is equally reliable, so it's important to assess the reliability of your sources. Whether you're gathering testimonial evidence, historical evidence, or documentary evidence, ask yourself the following questions to evaluate the information's credibility:

- *Is this source biased or impartial?* A biased source may present information in a way that favors their perspective, so it's important to consider whether the source has any vested interest in the outcome.
- *Is the information based on facts or opinions?* Facts are verifiable and objective, while opinions are subjective and open to interpretation. Be cautious when basing your conclusions solely on opinions.
- *Is the source consistent with other evidence?* Reliable evidence should be consistent with other credible sources. If a piece

of evidence contradicts everything else you've gathered, it may require further investigation.

- *Is the source qualified to provide this information?* Consider whether the person or entity providing the information has the necessary expertise or experience to be credible.

Avoiding Logical Fallacies

Logical fallacies are errors in reasoning that can undermine the validity of your argument or conclusion. To think critically, it's important to recognize and avoid these common false beliefs:

- **Ad Hominem:** Attacking the person making the argument rather than addressing the argument itself. For example, dismissing someone's opinion because of their background rather than evaluating their reasoning.
- **Straw Man:** Misrepresenting or oversimplifying someone else's argument in order to make it easier to attack. If someone says, *"I think we should consider budget cuts,"* and you respond with, *"So you want us to fire half the staff?"*, that's a straw-man fallacy.
- **False Dilemma (Either-Or Fallacy):** Presenting two extreme options as the only possible outcomes when there may be other alternatives. Saying something like, *"You're either with me or against me"* creates a false dichotomy.
- **Circular Reasoning:** When the conclusion of an argument is simply a restatement of the premise, without providing any new evidence. It might sound a bit like, *"This product is the best because it's better than all the others."*

By identifying and avoiding these fallacies, you can ensure that your reasoning is logical, coherent, and well-supported by evidence.

Weighing the Evidence

Once you've gathered and evaluated your evidence, it's important to weigh it in terms of relevance, reliability, and consistency. Not all evidence carries the same weight, and some pieces of evidence may be more significant than others. Here's how to weigh your evidence effectively:

- **Relevance:** Does the evidence directly address the question or issue at hand, or is it tangential? Evidence directly related to your inquiry should be given more weight than loosely connected evidence.
- **Reliability:** Is the source of the evidence trustworthy and credible? Reliable sources, such as direct observations, documented records, or expert testimony, should be given more weight than anecdotal or circumstantial evidence.
- **Consistency:** Is the evidence consistent with other pieces of evidence you've gathered? Evidence that aligns with other credible sources should be given more weight than evidence that contradicts everything else you know.

Weighing evidence helps you prioritize the most important and reliable information, leading to well-founded decisions.

The Power of Receipts in Real Life: Uncovering Truths in Personal Journeys

For the first part of this journey, we began by uncovering how easily assumptions can shape the way we see ourselves and the world around us. We explored how emotions influence our thinking, sometimes leading us to mistake feelings for facts. From there, we examined the toll of negative thought patterns and the way overthinking can drain energy, cloud judgment, and damage relationships.

Next, we turned to the foundations of building a receipt-based mindset—learning to pause, question, and gather evidence before drawing conclusions. We also considered the costs of living without receipts, recognizing how self-deception, unchecked biases, and misplaced confidence can silently steer our lives. Finally, we developed the skill of asking better questions, cultivating curiosity, and learning to search for truth through both internal reflection and external validation.

Now it's time to bring these ideas to life through the stories of four individuals—Rhonda, Sara, Ronald, and Carmen—each navigating unique struggles with self-deception, misplaced beliefs, and emotional challenges. Each character's journey reveals how their lives were shaped by their unexamined assumptions and emotions, and how learning to ask for receipts—the concrete, verifiable truth—helped them transform their thinking and, ultimately, their lives.

Each of these characters comes from different backgrounds with unique life experiences, but they all share one common struggle: living in a way that doesn't align with the truth. They operate on assumptions and fears rather than seeking out the evidence they need to make decisions based on reality. Through their stories, we'll see how asking the right questions, gathering evidence, and using critical thinking can lead to a more fulfilling, grounded life.

Rhonda: The Co-Parenting Dreamer

Background:

Rhonda is a 28-year-old single mother from Atlanta, Georgia. She works as a full-time nurse at a local hospital, and while she loves her profession, she often finds herself emotionally drained after long shifts. When Rhonda looks at her life, she sees strength and perseverance, but she also sees a lot of unresolved pain and disappointment, especially surrounding her past relationship with Marcus, the father of her son, Jamie.

Rhonda grew up in a family that valued traditional family structures. Her parents were married for 35 years, and despite some ups and downs, they presented a united front. Rhonda idolized her parents' marriage and believed that family was the most important thing in the world. When she met Marcus during her final year of nursing school, she thought she'd found someone with whom she could build that same kind of family life.

Marcus was charismatic and charming. He had a way of making Rhonda feel like she was the most important person in the world. He showered her with attention, and their relationship moved quickly. Within a year, they were living together, and shortly after, Rhonda became pregnant with Jamie. While their relationship was rocky even before Jamie's birth, Rhonda believed that starting a family would help solidify their bond.

However, reality set in quickly. Marcus was emotionally abusive, manipulative, and often absent. He had little interest in being a father, and Rhonda found herself raising Jamie mostly on her own. Even though Marcus's behavior ranged from indifference to outright hostility, Rhonda still hoped he'd one day step up and be the father Jamie deserved.

Rhonda's belief in Marcus's potential as a father was deeply rooted in her fear of failure. She didn't want to admit that her relationship with Marcus had been a mistake, nor did she want to face the stigma of being a single mother. Despite the evidence in front of her—Marcus's continued absence, lack of financial support, and empty promises—Rhonda chose to believe that if she just waited a little longer, things would change.

For three years, Rhonda juggled her demanding job as a nurse with the responsibilities of raising Jamie on her own. She was constantly exhausted, emotionally drained, and felt like she was carrying the weight of the world on her shoulders. Her friends and family expressed concern about Marcus's lack of involvement, but Rhonda dismissed their worries. She didn't want to admit that the father of her child was unreliable and uninterested in their son's life.

Rhonda continued to invite Marcus to Jamie's birthday parties, school events, and doctor's appointments, hoping that he'd take an interest. But each time, Marcus made excuses or simply didn't show up. This cycle of hope and disappointment took a toll on Rhonda, but she couldn't bring herself to let go of the idea that one day, Marcus would change.

Turning Point: Learning to Ask for Receipts

The turning point for Rhonda came during a routine therapy session. She'd been seeing a therapist for several months, primarily to help her manage the stress of single motherhood and the emotional toll of Marcus's ongoing absence. During one session, Rhonda was venting about Marcus's latest broken promise—he'd told Jamie that he would take him to the zoo, but he never showed up. Jamie had been devastated, and Rhonda found herself scrambling to make up for Marcus's absence once again.

As Rhonda talked about the situation, her therapist asked her a simple but profound question: *"What evidence do you have that Marcus is capable of being the father you want him to be?"* Rhonda paused. She'd never really thought about it that way before. She'd been operating on the assumption that Marcus had the potential to be a good father, but when she stopped to think about it, she realized that she had no concrete evidence to support that belief.

For the first time, Rhonda began to examine the facts. She looked back at the past three years and saw a pattern of inconsistency, broken promises, and indifference. Marcus had *never* made a sustained effort to be part of Jamie's life. He rarely visited, didn't contribute financially, and only seemed to reach out when it was convenient for him. There was no receipt to suggest that Marcus would ever change.

Rhonda's therapist encouraged her to start asking herself, *Where's my receipts?* whenever she found herself holding onto hope that Marcus would step up. By focusing on the evidence rather than what she wanted to believe, Rhonda began to see the situation more clearly.

This new way of thinking was uncomfortable at first. Rhonda had spent years holding onto the belief that Marcus would eventually become the father Jamie needed and letting go of that hope felt like admitting defeat. But as she continued to ask for receipts, she realized that her belief in Marcus was based on fear, not reality. She feared being judged as a single mother, feared that Jamie would grow up without a father figure, and feared that she'd be seen as a failure for not being able to "fix" her family.

Once Rhonda began to accept the truth, she felt a sense of relief. She no longer had to carry the emotional burden of trying to make Marcus into someone he wasn't. She stopped inviting him to Jamie's events, stopped expecting him to contribute financially, and set clear boundaries about his involvement in their lives. While this decision was difficult, it allowed Rhonda to focus on building a stable, loving home for Jamie without the constant disappointment of Marcus's broken promises.

As Rhonda embraced this new mindset, she found that her relationship with Jamie had improved. She was more present and emotionally available for him because she wasn't preoccupied with trying to manage Marcus's absence. Rhonda realized that she could be a strong, capable mother on her own, and she didn't need to rely on Marcus to validate her as a parent.

Rhonda's journey wasn't easy, but by learning to look for receipts, she was able to let go of the fantasy of a perfect family and embrace the reality of her situation. She found strength in accepting the truth and discovered that she was capable of creating a fulfilling life for herself and Jamie without needing Marcus to be part of the picture.

Sara: The Suspicious Wife

Background:

Sara is a 36-year-old stay-at-home mom living in suburban Detroit, Michigan. She's been married to her husband, Mark, for ten years, and together they have two children, ages eight and five. On the surface, Sara's life seems ideal. Mark is a successful attorney who works hard to provide for their family, and he's a loving and attentive husband. Sara has the freedom to stay home with their children, volunteer at their school, and pursue hobbies like gardening and photography.

But beneath the surface, Sara has always struggled with insecurities, particularly in her relationship with Mark. Even though Mark consistently shows his love and commitment to their family, Sara can't shake the feeling that something is wrong. She frequently worries that Mark is having an affair, even though there's no evidence to support her suspicions. Whenever Mark doesn't initiate sex or seems distracted, Sara assumes the worst.

Sara's insecurity is rooted in her past. Growing up, she watched her parents' marriage deteriorate due to her father's infidelity. Her father's affair shattered her mother, and Sara witnessed firsthand the emotional devastation it caused. From a young age, Sara learned that relationships were fragile, and that betrayal could happen at any moment. As a result, she developed a deep fear of abandonment and a tendency to be hyper-vigilant in her relationships.

When Sara married Mark, she thought she'd found a safe haven. Mark was everything her father wasn't—faithful, reliable, and loving. But as the years went on, Sara's insecurities resurfaced. She couldn't help but compare Mark to her father, and she began to see signs of infidelity in even the smallest actions. If Mark came home late from work, Sara's mind would race, wondering if he'd been with another woman. If he didn't compliment her appearance, she assumed he no longer found her attractive.

Sara's constant need for reassurance put a strain on the marriage. While Mark was patient and understanding, he grew frustrated with Sara's baseless accusations. He reassured her time and time again that he was committed to their family, but Sara couldn't let go of her suspicions. She often found herself scanning Mark's phone for evidence, interpreting his every move through the lens of her fear of betrayal.

Turning Point: Facing the Receipts

The turning point for Sara came after yet another argument about Mark's supposed infidelity. Mark had been working long hours on a big case, and by the time he got home, he was often too tired to be intimate. One night, when Mark came home late and went straight to bed without initiating sex, Sara exploded. She accused him of cheating, convinced that his lack of interest in her was a sign that he was getting his needs met elsewhere.

Mark, exhausted and hurt, asked Sara a pointed question: *"What evidence do you have that I'm cheating on you?"* Sara was taken aback. She'd never really stopped to think about it that way. Her accusations stemmed entirely from her fears and insecurities, not concrete proof.

How to Break Free from Confirmative Thinking

As she sat in silence, Sara began to reflect on Mark's actions. He came home every night and engaged with his family, even when he was tired. He called her during the day to check in and planned weekly date nights. He was present and engaged with their children and always made time for family dinners. There was no receipt to suggest that Mark was cheating. In fact, the evidence pointed to the opposite—Mark was a loving, faithful husband who was simply tired from the demands of his job.

Sara's realization hit her hard. She'd been operating on assumptions, allowing her past trauma and insecurities to dictate her perception of reality. The more she thought about it, the more she saw how unfair her accusations were. Mark had done nothing to deserve her suspicion, and yet she'd been punishing him for something her father had done years ago.

Determined to change, Sara started asking herself, *Where's my receipts?* before making any accusations or assumptions about Mark's behavior. Each time she felt her insecurities creeping in, she'd pause and ask herself if there was any actual evidence to support her fears. More often than not, the answer was no.

By focusing on the facts—Mark's consistent presence, his affection, and his commitment to their family—Sara began to rebuild trust in the marriage. She realized that her suspicions were unfounded and that they were rooted in her own unresolved trauma, not in anything Mark had done. This shift in perspective allowed Sara to let go of her fears and appreciate the love and stability that Mark provided.

As Sara continued to practice looking for receipts, her relationship with Mark improved dramatically. The arguments about infidelity stopped, and Sara was able to enjoy her marriage without constantly worrying about betrayal. She learned that trust wasn't just about believing in her husband—it was about believing in the evidence of his love and commitment.

Ronald: The People Pleaser

Background:

Ronald is a 32-year-old financial analyst living in Manhattan, New York. He works at a prestigious investment firm and is considered one of the rising stars in his company. From the outside, Ronald's life seems perfect—he has a high-paying job, lives in a luxury apartment, and drives an expensive car. His family, friends, and coworkers see him as a success, and Ronald works hard to maintain that image.

But underneath the surface, Ronald is struggling. He suffers from imposter syndrome, constantly feeling like he doesn't belong in his high-powered job. Even though he consistently receives positive feedback from his supervisors, Ronald is plagued by the fear that he will be exposed as a fraud. He works nine to ten hours a day, often staying up late to prove to himself and others that he deserves his position. While his colleagues leave at 5 p.m., Ronald stays until 7 or 8, hoping that his extra effort will be noticed.

Ronald's need for approval doesn't stop at work. He's a people-pleaser in every area of his life. He can't say no to his family, even when it means sacrificing his own financial stability. Whenever a family member asks for money, Ronald agrees, even if he doesn't have it to give. He's afraid that if he says no, his family will think he's selfish or that he's struggling financially, which would shatter the image of success he's worked so hard to maintain.

This constant need to please others is exhausting for Ronald. He feels like he's always "on"—always trying to prove himself but never feeling like he's good enough. He's constantly stressed, both mentally and financially, but he doesn't know how to break free from the expectations he feels are placed on him.

Turning Point: Confronting the Reality of His Actions

The turning point for Ronald came when he found himself overdrawn in his bank account after lending money to his cousin for the third time in a year. Ronald had been struggling to save for a down payment on a house, but every time he got close, a family member would ask for financial help, and Ronald would feel obligated to help. He couldn't bear the thought of his family seeing him as selfish or unsuccessful, and so he always said yes, even when it hurt him financially.

One day, Ronald's therapist asked him a simple question: *"What evidence do you have that lending money or working extra hours makes people respect you more?"* This question hit Ronald like a ton of bricks. He realized that he'd been operating under the assumption that saying yes to everyone would earn him respect and approval, but when he stopped to think about it, he realized that there was no concrete evidence to support that belief.

Ronald started asking himself, *Where's my receipts?* whenever he felt the urge to work extra hours or lend money he didn't have. He looked at the evidence: his coworkers didn't notice or care that he stayed late, his boss had never mentioned it, and his colleagues were getting promoted without putting in extra time. As for his family, Ronald realized that they never asked for the money—he'd just always offered it out of fear of judgment. When he stopped offering, nothing changed. His family still loved him, and no one thought less of him.

By looking for receipts, Ronald was able to see that his need to please others was based on his own insecurities, not on reality. He began setting boundaries at work and with his family, and while it was uncomfortable at first, he soon found that his relationships improved. His coworkers respected him for his work, not for the extra hours he put in, and his family valued him for who he was, not for the money he gave.

As Ronald embraced this new mindset, he felt a sense of relief. He no longer had to carry the burden of constantly trying to prove himself. He realized that he was already enough, and he didn't need to work extra hours or lend money to be valued. By focusing on the evidence, Ronald was able to let go of his need for approval and find peace in knowing that he was respected and loved for who he was, not for what he did.

Carmen: The Love Skeptic

Background:

Carmen is a 45-year-old marketing executive living in Houston, Texas. She's built a successful career for herself, working her way up from an entry-level position to a leadership role at a major advertising firm. Carmen is fiercely independent, self-sufficient, and proud of the life she's built. But despite her professional success, there's one area of Carmen's life that feels empty—her romantic relationships.

Carmen has been single for most of her adult life. She's had a few short-lived relationships, but none of them ever turned into anything serious. Over time, Carmen began to convince herself that love just wasn't in the cards for her. She believed that because she didn't fit society's standards of beauty—she felt a little overweight, had never been one to dress up or wear makeup, and preferred comfort over fashion—she'd never meet a man who truly loved her.

As the years went on, Carmen became increasingly bitter toward the idea of love. She told herself that she didn't need a relationship and that she was better off alone. But deep down, Carmen longed for companionship. She watched her friends get married and start families, and while she outwardly acted indifferent, she couldn't shake the feeling that something was missing in her life.

Carmen's bitterness stemmed from a deep-seated fear of rejection. She'd been hurt in the past, and rather than risk being hurt again, she built up walls around her heart. She told herself that she didn't want a relationship, that she was too busy with her career, and that she didn't need anyone to complete her. But the truth was that Carmen was lonely. She wanted love, but she didn't believe it was possible for her.

Turning Point: Changing the Narrative

The turning point for Carmen came during a conversation with one of her closest friends who'd recently gotten engaged. Carmen had been avoiding the topic of relationships for years, but her friend gently asked her, *"Why do you believe that love isn't for you?"* Carmen shrugged and gave her usual response: "I'm just not the type of woman men fall in love with."

Her friend challenged her: *"What evidence do you have to support that?"* Carmen paused. She'd never thought about it that way before. Her belief that she wasn't lovable was something she'd carried for so long without questioning it. As she reflected on her past relationships, Carmen realized that none of them had ended because of her appearance or weight. In fact, most of her relationships had ended because she'd pushed people away, afraid of getting too close and being rejected.

For the first time, Carmen began to ask herself, *Where's my receipts?*, when it came to her beliefs about love? She realized she'd been telling herself a story that wasn't based on evidence. She'd convinced herself that she wasn't worthy of love because of her appearance, but the truth was that she'd never given herself the chance to be loved.

Carmen started to challenge her negative beliefs about herself and her worthiness of love. She began to take small steps to open herself up to the possibility of a relationship. She joined a dating app, went on a few dates, and started to let go of the walls she'd built around her heart. While it wasn't easy, Carmen found that when she focused on the evidence—her kind nature, her successful career, and her capacity for love—she began to believe that she was deserving of a healthy, loving relationship.

The Empowering Practice of Living with Receipts

In this chapter, we've explored the critical skills of asking the right questions, gathering reliable evidence, and applying tools for critical thinking. These skills are at the heart of a receipt-based mindset—one that empowers you to navigate life's challenges with clarity, confidence, and a commitment to the truth.

As you continue to develop your receipt-based mindset, remember that the pursuit of truth is an ongoing journey. It requires curiosity, patience, and the courage to ask difficult questions. But by committing to this practice, you'll create a foundation of integrity and authenticity that'll serve you in every area of your life.

The practice of collecting receipts is a powerful tool in shaping our beliefs and actions, but it's not just about gathering evidence. The next step is learning to trust the process and our ability to navigate the complexities of life based on that evidence. In the upcoming chapter, we'll focus on how to turn down the noise of uncertainty, trust your decision-making process and move forward with confidence.

Chapter 7: Turning Off the Overthinking Machine

One of the key benefits of living a receipt-based life is its ability to help you shut off the constant cycle of overthinking. Overthinking is mentally exhausting, emotionally draining, and often leads to unnecessary anxiety. We all, at times, overthink. It's a mental habit that can disguise itself as productivity, responsibility, or even emotional intelligence. In reality, overthinking leaves us stuck, overwhelmed, and disconnected from what's true. When left unchecked, this mental noise becomes the background music of our lives—loud, distracting, and mentally suffocating.

This chapter is about learning how to quiet that noise. Specifically, it's about using receipt-based thinking to interrupt the loop of rumination, fear, and indecision. When you have no clear evidence to support or challenge your thoughts, your mind tends to fill in the blanks with worst-case scenarios. When you collect receipts—real, verifiable data—you see many of your worries are built on "what ifs" rather than facts.

We'll start by helping you recognize when you've done enough thinking. Then we'll address the most common overthinking trap: the endless cycle of "what ifs." Finally, you'll be introduced to a set of practical techniques—like mindfulness, cognitive defusion, and the five-minute rule—to help you stop spiraling and start moving forward. These techniques ground you in the present and create immediate mental space—not for deeper reflection, but to break the loop in real time.

How to Know When You've Done Enough Thinking

One of the biggest challenges for overthinkers is knowing when to stop. How do you know when you've thought something through enough to make a decision, take action, or let it go?

Overthinkers get stuck in endless analysis—trying to predict every outcome, prevent mistakes, or avoid discomfort. This excessive thinking wastes time and creates more stress.

A receipt-based mindset can help you recognize when you've done enough thinking. The idea is simple: if you've gathered the facts, assessed the evidence, and there's nothing new to consider, it's time to stop thinking and start acting. The following steps can help guide you in determining when you've done enough thinking.

Step 1: Gather the Receipts

Before you can stop thinking, you need to ensure that you've gathered all the necessary evidence. This doesn't mean endlessly searching or over-researching—it means gathering enough facts to make an informed decision.

Let's say you're considering a job change but feel stuck in a cycle of overthinking about whether to make the move. To stop the cycle, you need to focus on gathering relevant facts:

- What are the benefits and downsides of the new job?
- Does the new role align with your long-term career goals?
- How does the pay and work-life balance compare to your current job?

Once you have this information, you've gathered your receipts. This is where you should stop endless research and rumination.

Step 2: Ask, "*What New Information Could I Possibly Gain?*"

Once you've gathered the evidence, the next step is to ask yourself, "*What new information could I possibly gain by continuing to think about this?"* If the answer is nothing, then it's time to let it go. Overthinking happens because we believe more thinking will bring new insights, but once we've gathered the necessary information, that's rarely true.

Rhonda, (from the previous chapter) spent years overthinking her role as a co-parent, constantly replaying scenarios in her mind about how she might convince Marcus, Jamie's father, to be more present. She analyzed every interaction, hoping she could unlock the formula to change him, even though the receipts already showed a clear pattern of absence and broken promises. However, once Rhonda gathered the evidence—Marcus's continued absence, his failure to support their child, and his broken promises—she realized that no amount of further thinking was going to change the situation. She had all the receipts she needed to make a decision, and continuing to overthink only caused her more stress.

Step 3: Set a Decision-Making Deadline

Overthinking thrives in the absence of clear timelines. One way to stop overthinking is to set a decision-making deadline. Give yourself a specific amount of time to think about the issue, gather the facts, and then make a decision. A deadline forces focus and prevent endless analysis.

If you're deciding whether to move to a new city, give yourself a set amount of time—say, two weeks—to gather information, visit the area, and weigh the pros and cons. At the end of the two weeks, make a decision based on the facts you've collected. After that, stop rehashing the decision in your mind. Trust the process and let go of any further analysis.

Recognizing the Mental Loop of "What Ifs"

Overthinking often manifests in the form of "what if" scenarios. You might find yourself constantly asking:

- *What if I fail?*
- *What if I make the wrong decision?*
- *What if things don't turn out the way I want?*

While it's normal to consider outcomes before a decision, when the "what ifs" take over, you become paralyzed by indecision. The problem with "what if" thinking is that it's based on hypothetical situations that may or may not happen rather than on concrete evidence or facts.

Sara, (from the previous chapter) had long been strained by her insecurities and suspicions of infidelity. She had begun working on grounding herself in moments of doubt. Instead of being ruled by her fears, she practiced pausing when the "what ifs" crept in. She asked herself, *Where's my receipts* that Mark is unfaithful? The evidence—his steady presence, his commitment to family time, his daily check-ins—helped her see that her fears were rooted in insecurity, not reality. This was her first step in breaking free from the cycle of suspicion.

Why "What If" Thinking is So Powerful

Overthinking doesn't always show up as loud panic—it often whispers in the form of "what ifs." These quiet questions feel responsible or even necessary, as if worrying more will somehow protect us. In reality, "what if" thinking rarely leads to clarity. Instead, it creates fear-based hypotheticals that drain energy and cloud judgment. If we want to break the loop, we have to start by understanding why these thoughts feel so convincing in the first place.

Our brains are wired to focus on threats and risks, which is why "what if" thinking can feel so compelling. It's part of our survival instinct to anticipate danger, but when it becomes excessive, it leads to unnecessary stress. The key to breaking free from this mental loop is to differentiate between real risks (those backed by evidence) and imagined risks (those based on fear or uncertainty).

Ronald, (from the previous chapter) often found himself stuck in the "what if" loop. He constantly worried about what his family would think if he stopped lending them money. He asked himself, *"What if they stop respecting me? What if they think I'm selfish or broke?"* This mental loop kept him trapped in the cycle of people-pleasing. But when Ronald asked himself, *Where's my receipts?* he realized that there was no evidence to support his fears. His family had never questioned his generosity or viewed him negatively for setting boundaries.

How to Break the "What If" Cycle

The "what if" loop feeds on uncertainty, but clarity comes from evidence—not fear. When you pause to examine your thoughts, ask for receipts, and challenge unfounded predictions, you take back control from your overthinking mind. Breaking this cycle won't happen overnight, but with practice, you'll begin to trust your ability to navigate uncertainty without spiraling. The more you focus on what is, rather than what might be, the more peace you'll find in daily decisions.

Below are some strategies for breaking free from the "what if" loop and grounding yourself in reality:

- **Step 1: Identify the Hypothetical vs. the Real:** When you find yourself caught in a "what if" scenario, pause and ask yourself, *"Is this a real concern or a hypothetical fear?"* If it's a hypothetical fear, acknowledge it but don't let it control your thinking.

Instead of asking, *"What if I fail at this new project?"* reframe the question to *"What evidence do I have that I will fail?"* Focus on the facts—your past successes, your skills, and the support available to you. If there's no concrete evidence to suggest you'll fail, let go of the fear.

- **Step 2: Consider the Likelihood of Each "What If":** When overthinking, we often imagine the worst-case scenario. To stop this cycle, assess how likely each "what if" is to happen. Is the worst-case scenario *really* the most probable outcome?

  Carmen (from the previous chapter) often asked herself, *"What if no one ever loves me because of my weight?"* When she looked at the evidence, she realized that she'd been on dates, had friendships with people who valued her for who she was, and had never been rejected explicitly because of her appearance. The worst-case scenario she feared was unlikely, and by focusing on the receipts, she was able to break free from her negative thinking.

- **Step 3: Challenge the "What If" with Evidence:** The way to counter a "what if" is to ask for evidence. Whenever a "what if" thought arises, challenge it by asking, *"What proof do I have that this will happen?* If there's no substantial evidence, it's likely just an overthinking loop that you can dismiss.

  If you're worried about a social situation— *"What if no one likes me at the party?"* ask yourself, *"What evidence do I have that this will happen?"* Look at past experiences in which you've been in similar situations and found people were friendly and welcoming. Use this evidence to challenge the negative "what if."

Techniques to Quiet Overactive Thoughts

Even after gathering evidence and challenging "what if" scenarios, overthinking can still persist. For some people, overthinking has become such a habitual mental pattern that it's hard to quiet the mind, even when they know their thoughts are irrational or unproductive. In these cases, it's helpful to have practical techniques for calming overactive thoughts and bringing your mind back to the present.

Technique 1: Mindfulness & Grounding

One of the fastest ways to interrupt overthinking is to bring your awareness back to the present moment. When your mind races with worries or "what ifs," it's often because you're living in a future that hasn't happened—or replaying a past that's already over. In this chapter, mindfulness isn't about deep insight—it's about regaining control in the moment when thoughts are racing. Mindfulness offers a powerful antidote to this mental trap.

Mindfulness is paying attention to your thoughts, feelings, and surroundings without judgment. Rather than accepting every thought as fact, mindfulness teaches you to observe them as mental events—temporary and passing. This perspective shift alone can dramatically reduce the grip of anxious or spiraling thoughts.

A simple but effective way to practice mindfulness is through grounding, a technique that engages your five senses to reconnect you with the present moment. The goal isn't to stop thinking altogether—it's to recognize when your thoughts are pulling you into fear, assumption, or fantasy, and gently bring yourself back to what is real and verifiable in the here and now.

Grounding Exercise:

Step 1: Sit or stand comfortably and begin by taking a few deep, intentional breaths.

Step 2: Bring awareness to your five senses. Ask yourself:

- What do I see?
- What do I hear?
- What do I feel?
- What do I smell?
- What do I taste (if anything)?

Step 3: When a distracting or distressing thought enters your mind, acknowledge it without judgment—then gently redirect your focus back to your senses or your breath. Repeat this process as needed.

Sara often found herself spiraling with thoughts about her husband's behavior—interpreting his quietness as a sign of betrayal. Instead of verifying her assumptions with actual receipts (like direct communication), she would let the fear-fueled thoughts take over.

When Sara began practicing grounding exercises, she noticed a shift. The moment her mind started to wander into suspicion or fear, she'd pause, breathe deeply, and focused on the feeling of her hands on her lap or the texture of the chair beneath her. Over time, this mindful practice helped her step back from her thoughts and evaluate them more objectively. Instead of reacting from a place of panic, she could calm her nervous system and engage in more honest, evidence-based conversations with her husband.

Mindfulness and grounding don't erase your concerns—they give you the clarity and space to approach them from a grounded place. As you practice, you'll find it becomes easier to recognize the difference between a runaway thought and a grounded reality.

Mindfulness helps you anchor yourself in the present and interrupt overthinking in real time—but sometimes the thoughts that arise are persistent and emotionally charged, requiring a different approach. When those thoughts return again and again—despite your best efforts to stay grounded— it's not always enough to acknowledge them. You need a strategy for how to handle them. That's where cognitive defusion comes in.

While mindfulness and grounding help bring your attention back to the present, some thoughts still manage to linger— especially the ones that hit close to home. These thoughts tend to be emotionally charged and self-critical, and they can sneak past even your most mindful moments. When that happens, you need a tool that allows you to separate yourself from the thought altogether. That's where cognitive defusion comes in—a technique designed to loosen the grip of unhelpful thoughts by changing the way you relate to them.

Technique 2: Cognitive Defusion

Cognitive defusion is a technique rooted in Acceptance and Commitment Therapy (ACT) that teaches you how to step back from your thoughts instead of getting swept up in them. Rather than trying to fight or suppress unhelpful thoughts, defusion invites you to change your relationship to them—to see them not as facts but as temporary mental events.

It's common to get caught in the grip of negative self-talk: thoughts like *"I'm not good enough," "I'll never succeed,"* or *"People don't really like me."* These thoughts can feel so real and automatic that we accept them without question. But defusion helps you loosen their hold by shifting your internal dialogue. You begin to see that having a thought doesn't make it true.

One practical way to practice cognitive defusion is by adding the phrase: *"I'm having the thought that…"* before the belief. This small change helps you observe the thought rather than identify with it. It gives you space to respond instead of reacting.

Exercise: Cognitive Defusion Worksheet:
Let's try putting this into practice.

Purpose:
To help you create space between yourself and your thoughts so you can observe them without becoming entangled in them. This shift will reduce their emotional intensity and allow for more grounded, intentional responses.

Instructions:

1. Identify a repetitive or distressing thought you've been struggling with.
2. Write it down exactly as it appears in your mind.
3. Now, rephrase it by saying: *"I'm having the thought that…"* before the statement.
4. Repeat it slowly out loud. Say it again in a silly voice or imagine the thought floating by on a cloud—anything to disrupt the seriousness with which the mind delivers it.
5. Reflect on how this shifts the emotional weight of the thought.
6. Finally, make a plan for how you will apply this practice in the future when similar thoughts arise.

Ronald, who struggled with imposter syndrome and people-pleasing, often thought that saying yes to everyone—whether at work or with family—proved his worth. He worked late, lent money, and stretched himself thin, but the evidence rarely supported his belief that these sacrifices earned him the respect he longed for.

Cognitive defusion teaches you that not every thought needs a reaction. Some thoughts just need space—and perspective. By practicing defusion, you create mental flexibility to respond to life from a place of clarity instead of fear.

Even with mindfulness and cognitive defusion in your toolkit, there will be times when a decision still feels impossible to make. That's because overthinking often disguises itself as being thorough or just wanting to be sure, when in reality, it's just a delay tactic rooted in fear. You gather receipts, challenge your thoughts, but then freeze—unable to move forward. In these moments, you don't need more analysis; you need a boundary. That's where the five-minute rule comes in. It's a structured way to interrupt the cycle and take action with confidence.

Technique 3: The Five-Minute Rule

For chronic overthinkers, it's easy to become paralyzed by indecision or the need to analyze every outcome. The five-minute rule is a helpful tool for interrupting this pattern. The idea is simple: give yourself five minutes to think about an issue. After the five minutes are up, you must stop, make a decision, or take action based on the information you have.

This rule forces you to focus only on the most relevant information and helps you avoid the trap of over-analyzing every possible detail. It also helps you practice trusting your instincts and the evidence you've already gathered.

Try the following exercise to practice using the five-minute rule when indecision strikes.

Exercise: Five-Minute Rule Worksheet:

- Set a timer for five minutes the next time you find yourself overthinking a problem.
- During those five minutes, focus on the most important information or receipts.
- Once the timer goes off, stop thinking about the issue and make a decision or take action based on what you know.

Carmen often overthought social situations, especially around dating. She'd spend hours obsessing over whether she should respond to a message or go on a date, paralyzed by thoughts such as, *"What if he doesn't like me? What if I'm not good enough?"* Carmen began using the five-minute rule to stop this cycle. She'd give herself five minutes to think about the situation, review any relevant information, and then make a decision. This simple rule helped her take action without getting lost in unnecessary self-doubt.

Each time Carmen used the five-minute rule, she gained confidence in her ability to take action without being paralyzed by fear. She realized that her overthinking wasn't protecting her—it was keeping her stuck. By limiting her decision-making time and focusing only on the receipts she had, Carmen began practicing courage instead of avoidance.

Using the five-minute rule is a form of self-trust. It teaches you that you don't need to have every answer before you move forward. You simply need enough verified information— enough receipts—to make a reasonable decision. The goal isn't perfection; it's progress. And by practicing this method, you start to build confidence in your ability to take action, even amid uncertainty.

Of course, even after you've made a decision, lingering thoughts can still swirl in your mind. Sometimes, the mental clutter doesn't come from uncertainty—it comes from having too much to process at once. When your thoughts feel tangled or repetitive, the best way to sort through them is to get them out of your head and onto the page. That's where writing to release mental clutter becomes a powerful tool.

Technique 4: Writing to Release Mental Clutter

Sometimes, the mind just needs a place to unload. While tools like mindfulness or decision-making frameworks can help interrupt mental loops, writing offers a different kind of relief—one that doesn't require resolution, just release. Here, writing serves as a mental release valve—not to deeply analyze or reflect, but to get overwhelming thoughts out of your head and onto the page. When your thoughts feel too loud or too layered, journaling becomes a way to untangle them. Writing allows you to see thoughts more clearly, track emotional patterns, and give form to mental noise that might otherwise stay stuck on repeat.

Journaling can be an effective way to quiet overactive thoughts. Writing down your thoughts helps externalize them, making them feel less overwhelming. Writing can also help you process emotions, sort through conflicting thoughts, and see patterns that might not be obvious when the thoughts are trapped inside your head.

Journaling Exercise:

- Spend 10–15 minutes each day writing whatever is on your mind. Don't worry about structure or grammar—just let your thoughts flow.
- After you've finished writing, review what you've written and highlight any recurring themes or thoughts that seem to be contributing to your overthinking.
- Use this writing process as a way to clarify your thoughts and focus on the evidence you've gathered.

Rhonda started journaling as a way to release her overactive thoughts. Each time she felt overwhelmed by worry or frustration, she'd write down her thoughts, concerns, and emotions. By reviewing her journal entries, Rhonda was able to see how much mental energy she'd been wasting on overanalyzing Marcus's behavior, which helped her refocus on the facts: Marcus was unreliable, and overthinking wouldn't change that.

Overthinking can feel like an endless cycle, but with the right tools and mindset, you can quiet your mind and focus on the facts. By adopting a receipt-based approach to your thoughts, you can break free from the mental loops of "what ifs" and endless analysis. You don't have to be trapped in overthinking—there's a way to shift your focus to reality, make decisions based on evidence, and free yourself from the mental clutter.

Knowing when you've done enough thinking, recognizing when you're caught in a loop, and applying practical techniques to calm your mind are all essential steps in shutting off the overthinking machine. By practicing these strategies, you'll be able to make decisions with more confidence, reduce unnecessary stress, and live more grounded in reality.

Remember, the key to quieting your mind isn't about suppressing your thoughts or forcing yourself to stop thinking altogether—it's about grounding your thinking in truth, focusing on what you can control, and trusting the evidence you've gathered. The receipts guide you, and by relying on them, you can find peace of mind and break free from the exhausting cycle of overthinking.

As we develop a system for validating our receipts, it's important to recognize that true clarity comes not only from external evidence but also from internal reflection. The next chapter will explore how self-reflection can help you track your thoughts, beliefs, and actions, creating a deeper awareness that strengthens your internal receipts. Honing this practice builds the insight needed to navigate challenges with more confidence and objectivity.

Chapter 8: The Power of Self-Reflection: Building Internal Receipts

Internal receipts are proof points that come from within, grounded in personal insights, self-awareness, and reflection. These are realizations gained from consistently checking in with ourselves to track thoughts, beliefs, and actions over time. This chapter will focus on how self-reflection allows us to build internal receipts, helping us live more authentically and with greater clarity.

We'll explore how regular self-reflection creates a grounded sense of self, making it easier to spot inconsistencies, correct mistaken beliefs, and identify areas where we're deceiving ourselves. By developing internal accountability, we can confront hard truths about ourselves with honesty, ultimately leading to personal growth and emotional resilience.

We'll also cover the power of self-reflection, the role of internal receipts in personal accountability, and practical exercises like journaling, meditation, and self-questioning. Unlike in the previous chapter, where these tools quieted mental spirals, here they deepen self-awareness and uncover the patterns shaping your beliefs and behaviors.

What Are Internal Receipts?

Internal receipts are the truths we uncover about ourselves through introspection and self-awareness. Unlike external receipts, which rely on objective evidence from the outside world, internal receipts are gathered by reflecting on our inner experiences, emotions, and reactions. These internal checks are essential because they provide insight into who we are, how we think, and why we behave the way we do.

Self-deception can be subtle, often rooted in unconscious patterns of thinking, biases, or unresolved emotions. Through self-reflection, we shine a light on these hidden aspects of ourselves, giving us the opportunity to challenge unhelpful thought patterns, beliefs, or behaviors. Internal receipts provide evidence that helps realign our self-perception with reality. An example would be:

- **Belief:** *"I'm always calm under pressure."*
- **Internal Receipt:** After reflecting on a recent situation in which you felt overwhelmed, you realize that, in fact, you struggle to stay calm in stressful moments.

This reflection reveals a truth about yourself that you may have previously ignored or been unaware of, offering an opportunity for growth and adjustment.

The Role of Self-Reflection in Building Internal Receipts

Self-reflection is a conscious process of looking inward, assessing your thoughts, feelings, actions, and motivations. This practice enables you to observe patterns of behavior and recognize when you're aligning with your true values—or when you're *not*. When done regularly, self-reflection helps create a more consistent and authentic version of yourself because it brings to light internal discrepancies that may otherwise go unnoticed.

Many people struggle with self-reflection because it requires honesty, vulnerability, and the willingness to confront uncomfortable truths. However, without this practice, we risk falling into patterns of self-deception, blaming external circumstances for internal problems or staying stagnant in behaviors that no longer serve us.

Rhonda began journaling as part of her self-reflection. Instead of only writing about Marcus's absence, she started asking herself deeper questions: *"Why do I believe I've failed if Marcus doesn't show up? How does my family's 'traditional marriage' example shape my fear of being a single mother?"* These reflections revealed that her pain wasn't just about Marcus—it was about her own internalized belief that her worth as a parent depended on him.

Ronald also began using self-reflection to track his people-pleasing patterns. Instead of only focusing on how others perceived his long hours, he started asking himself deeper questions: *"What proof do I have that staying late actually earns me respect? Why do I believe saying no makes me selfish?"* These reflections revealed that his drive wasn't about ambition—it was about fear of rejection. With internal receipts, Ronald began to separate genuine work ethic from the pressure of constantly proving himself

Practical Exercises for Developing Self-Reflection

Self-reflection doesn't happen by accident—it's a habit that needs to be developed with intention and regular practice. There are several effective methods for cultivating this skill, each of which encourages you to slow down, examine your thoughts and feelings, and develop insights into your internal world. Below are some practical exercises that can help you build a consistent habit of self-reflection.

Exercise: Journaling for Clarity & Insight Worksheet

Journaling is one of the most effective tools for self-reflection because it puts thoughts and emotions into words, making them easier to analyze. Writing gives your thoughts structure, which forces you to articulate ideas clearly. This helps you track patterns over time, revealing insights into your beliefs, behaviors, and emotional responses that may not have been obvious initially.

Self-reflection isn't just a feel-good buzzword—it's a core practice for gathering internal receipts. When you reflect, you give yourself the chance to step outside the rush of daily thoughts and feelings and ask: *"What's really going on in my mind, and is it helping or hurting me?"* Without this pause, it's easy to operate on autopilot, letting unchallenged beliefs dictate your decisions and emotions.

The good news is that self-reflection is a skill—and like any skill, it can be cultivated. The following exercise is a practical tool to help you slow down, tune in, and begin identifying patterns in your inner dialogue that you may not have noticed before.

Journal Prompts for Internal Receipts:

- What have I been telling myself about a particular situation? Is it true?
- When did I last feel proud of myself, and why?
- What's one recurring thought or belief that may not be serving me?
- In what ways do I feel aligned with my values, and in what ways do I feel disconnected?

Carmen, who believed that love wasn't for her, could very effectively use journaling to explore her thoughts about relationships. Writing daily about isolation, bitterness, and fear of rejection would help her confront the belief that she wasn't worthy of love. This process would allow Carmen to gather internal receipts about how her thoughts had shaped her emotional reality, and she could then work to challenge those thoughts with compassion.

Through journaling, Carmen confronted the belief that her appearance made her unworthy of love. She noticed that her harshest thoughts weren't backed by receipts but by comparisons to unrealistic standards. Seeing this in her own writing gave her an internal receipt: the barrier wasn't her lovability, but her fear of rejection

Journaling may seem simple, but it's one of the most transformative practices you can adopt. It creates a paper trail of growth, helping you revisit thoughts with greater honesty, clarity, and insight. Each time you write, you gather more internal receipts—evidence of who you are becoming, not just who you've been told you are.

As you continue exploring your internal world, keep in mind: self-reflection without self-compassion can quickly turn into self-criticism.

Exercise: Meditation for Emotional Awareness

While journaling brings structure to your thoughts, meditation offers something just as important—stillness. In a world that rarely slows down, giving yourself permission to sit, breathe, and simply *observe* is a radical act of self-awareness. Meditation creates the mental space needed to notice your inner dialogue as it arises, without immediately reacting to it or labeling it as truth.

Meditation is a powerful tool for self-reflection because it cultivates awareness of thoughts and emotions without judgment. When you meditate, you observe your mental and emotional state in real-time, which allows you to see patterns of thinking and feeling as they arise. This practice helps you develop a deeper understanding of your internal world, allowing you to gather internal receipts more easily.

Sara also began using meditation as a way to observe her emotional spikes. She noticed that her anxiety flared most when Mark came home quiet or distracted. Sitting with those feelings showed her that the panic wasn't evidence of betrayal but a residue of her father's infidelity years earlier. This reflection became an internal receipt: her fear belonged to the past, not to Mark.

This next exercise is designed to help you tune into your emotional landscape without judgment, building the kind of internal clarity that allows your internal receipts to surface naturally.

Mindfulness Meditation Practice:

- **Step 1:** Find a quiet space and sit comfortably. Close your eyes and take a few deep breaths to center yourself.
- **Step 2:** Focus on your breath as it moves in and out of your body. If your mind starts to wander, gently guide it back to your breath.
- **Step 3:** Notice any thoughts, emotions, or physical sensations that arise during your meditation. Don't judge them—just observe them.
- **Step 4:** After your meditation, take a few minutes to reflect on what you noticed. Were there any recurring thoughts or emotions? How did you feel throughout the practice?

By regularly practicing meditation, you develop a heightened sense of awareness about your thoughts and feelings, making it easier to recognize when you're falling into negative patterns or self-deception.

The power of meditation isn't in achieving a blank mind—it's in learning how to observe your mind without judgment. Each time you sit in stillness, you strengthen your ability to catch distorted thinking before it becomes a belief. You become less reactive, more curious, and more attuned to what's real.

With tools like journaling and meditation, you've begun the process of observing your thoughts and emotional patterns more clearly. But self-questioning takes it a step further. It doesn't just help you notice your thoughts—it challenges them. It puts them on the witness stand and asks, *"Is this true, or just something I've been telling myself?"*

Exercise: Self-Questioning Worksheet

Self-questioning is an essential part of self-reflection, helping you probe your thoughts and beliefs to uncover deeper truths. This process means asking open-ended questions that challenge assumptions, uncover hidden motivations, and gather evidence about your internal state. Self-questioning leads to the development of internal receipts by encouraging you to assess the validity of your thoughts, feelings, and actions.

This reflective practice gives you an opportunity to challenge beliefs you've long accepted, even if they no longer serve you. It's not about criticism—it's about becoming a curious investigator of your inner world. When done regularly, self-questioning becomes one of the most powerful tools for collecting internal receipts and breaking free from limiting narratives.

Use the following prompts to start challenging your assumptions and digging beneath the surface of your automatic thoughts.

Examples of Self-Reflective Questions:

1. What beliefs am I holding onto that may no longer be true?
2. What am I avoiding confronting about myself, and why?
3. What patterns keep showing up in my life, and what are they trying to teach me?
4. How am I contributing to the current challenges I'm facing?
5. What do I need to let go of in order to grow?

Ronald could use self-questioning to explore his imposter syndrome. By asking, *"What proof do I have that I don't belong here?"* or *"Why do I feel like I'm not enough despite my success?"* he'd begin to gather internal receipts that debunk his belief in inadequacy.

The more willing you are to question yourself, the more equipped you become to evolve. Self-questioning creates a habit of internal accountability—one that helps you respond to life with greater clarity, purpose, and emotional maturity. Each pause to ask *why* creates a chance to break a pattern, rewrite a belief, or reclaim truth.

Building Internal Accountability & Clarity

One of the key benefits of developing internal receipts through self-reflection is that it leads to greater internal accountability. When you clearly understand your thoughts, motivations, and patterns, you can take full responsibility for your actions and decisions. This accountability builds integrity because you're no longer deceiving yourself or making excuses for behavior misaligned with your values.

Internal receipts also help you build clarity about your goals, desires, and boundaries. The more you reflect, the more you understand what you truly want and need, which makes it easier to make decisions that serve your authentic self rather than decisions based on external pressures or old patterns.

Rhonda, who held onto the belief that Marcus would eventually become a reliable father, could use self-reflection to create internal accountability. By regularly checking in, she'd see her hope in Marcus's change wasn't backed by evidence. This internal clarity would empower her to stop expecting Marcus to show up and instead focus on building a stable life for herself and her son Jamie based on the truth of the situation.

Using Internal Receipts to Spot Self-Deception

As described in chapter 5, self-deception is one of the biggest barriers to personal growth. It occurs when we convince ourselves of something that isn't true because it's more comfortable or less painful than facing reality. This often leads to stagnation, dissatisfaction, and emotional distress because we're living in a way that isn't aligned with the truth.

Internal receipts help us spot and address self-deception by forcing us to confront inconsistencies between our beliefs and behaviors. Regular self-reflection makes it easier to see where we might be lying to ourselves, avoiding the truth, or holding onto outdated narratives.

Carmen's belief that she wasn't worthy of love was self-deception. Reflecting on past relationships, she'd gather receipts showing her belief was based on fear rather than evidence. She'd see that her fear of rejection had led her to push people away before they could reject her. This realization would allow Carmen to stop deceiving herself and open up to the possibility of love.

The Ongoing Practice of Self-Reflection

Building internal receipts is a lifelong process. It requires regular practice, honesty, and a commitment to self-growth. The more you practice self-reflection, the easier it becomes to live aligned with your true self and make decisions based on both external and internal evidence.

By integrating practices like journaling, meditation, and self-questioning into your life, you'll develop greater self-awareness, emotional resilience, and clarity. Over time, this will help you spot inconsistencies in your beliefs and actions, allowing you to make adjustments that bring you closer to living a life grounded in truth.

The real power of self-reflection lies in how it holds you accountable to yourself. Internal receipts provide the proof you need to ensure that your thoughts, beliefs, and actions are aligned with reality. Committing to this practice frees you from self-deception, helps you embrace your authentic self, and make choices that lead to lasting fulfillment.

This chapter explored the importance of self-reflection and building internal receipts to deepen self-understanding. But self-reflection alone isn't enough to navigate life's complexities. Next, we'll expand to external receipts—objective evidence and feedback from the world around us. Integrating these perspectives offers a more balanced view, complementing your internal receipts and guiding decisions more effectively.

Chapter 9: External Receipts: Tying Together Internal & External Receipts

In the last chapter, we explored the significance of internal receipts—the truths we uncover through self-reflection, personal insight, and introspection. But internal receipts alone simply aren't enough. For a more comprehensive and grounded approach to life, we must also consider *external receipts*—the feedback, evidence, and observations we gather from the world around us.

External receipts provide the objective information we need to validate or challenge our internal perceptions. They give us a reality check when we're distorting the truth or slipping into self-deception. When internal and external receipts are used together, they create a balanced, holistic view that helps us align our thoughts, beliefs, and actions with the world around us.

In this chapter, we'll explore how to gather and interpret external receipts, the importance of feedback from others, and how to integrate both kinds of receipts to create a well-rounded, authentic perspective.

What Are External Receipts?

External receipts are the tangible, observable evidence we gather from the outside world. These include feedback from others, performance evaluations, measurable outcomes, or other objective data showing how we're perceived and how our actions affect the world.

While internal receipts come from within, external receipts provide confirmation (or contradiction) from an outside perspective. They help us ground our internal beliefs in reality by showing us how our behavior, choices, and interactions are seen by others. At times, we might believe that we're excellent communicators, but if our coworkers frequently express confusion or frustration during meetings, that's an external receipt telling us that our internal belief may not be entirely accurate.

External receipts are crucial for avoiding blind spots, challenging cognitive biases, and ensuring that our internal world aligns with the reality of our external experiences.

Gathering External Receipts: The Role of Feedback

One of the most valuable external receipts is feedback from others. Feedback is essential because it provides an outside perspective on how our actions and decisions are interpreted. Without feedback, we risk operating in a bubble in which we only rely on our own interpretations of reality—interpretations that can often be distorted by biases, emotions, or limited perspectives.

However, many people are uncomfortable with feedback because it can feel critical or confrontational. But learning to seek and accept feedback is essential for personal growth and self-awareness.

How to Seek Meaningful Feedback

- **Ask for Specific Observations:** Vague feedback like you're doing a great job, or you need to improve isn't particularly helpful. When seeking external receipts, ask for specific feedback that addresses particular actions or behaviors. For instance, instead of asking, *"How am I doing at work?"* ask, *"Can you provide feedback on how I handled the last team meeting?"*
- **Seek Feedback from a Variety of Sources:** External receipts should come from multiple perspectives to provide a well-rounded view. Relying solely on one person's

opinion can lead to a skewed perception. Gather feedback from different people in your life—colleagues, friends, family members, and even mentors or coaches.

- **Be Open to Constructive Criticism:** Bear in mind that external receipts aren't always positive. Sometimes, they reveal areas where we need to improve or where we've fallen short. It's important to approach feedback with openness and humility, recognizing that even critical feedback can be an opportunity for growth.
- **Use Feedback to Challenge Internal Beliefs:** Once you've gathered feedback, compare it to your internal receipts. Are there any discrepancies between how you see yourself and how others see you? Use feedback as a mirror to reflect on where you might need to adjust your internal perceptions.

Ronald believed that his coworkers saw him as diligent and hard-working because of the long hours he put in at the office. But when he gathered external feedback, he learned that his coworkers saw his extra hours as unnecessary and believed that he was overcompensating. This external receipt contradicted Ronald's internal belief that working longer hours earned him more respect, allowing him to adjust his approach.

Objective Measures as External Receipts

In addition to feedback, there are many objective external receipts that can provide us with valuable insights into our performance, behavior, or progress. These are the measurable outcomes and data points that show us whether we're moving in the right direction. Examples include:

- **Work Performance Metrics:** Sales numbers, productivity levels, or customer satisfaction scores can provide clear external receipts about your professional performance.

- **Health and Fitness Data:** Weight, blood pressure, or fitness tracking data are external receipts that reflect the effectiveness of your health habits.
- **Academic Grades or Test Scores:** These are objective measures of academic performance, which can provide a clear indication of where improvement is needed.

The key to using objective external receipts is to view them with balance. It's important not to define your entire self-worth by these external measures but rather to use them as valuable data points that can inform your growth and decisions.

Carmen, who'd long believed she wasn't capable of maintaining a healthy lifestyle, started monitoring her daily exercise and eating habits. Over time, her fitness tracking app provided external receipts in the form of real data—her stamina increased, her energy levels improved, and her weight stabilized. These external receipts validated Carmen's efforts, proving her changes were effective.

Just as her fitness data proved her physical progress, Carmen also began paying attention to relational feedback. Friends and colleagues regularly affirmed her warmth, humor, and kindness. These external receipts helped Carmen see that others valued her for qualities she had long dismissed, further challenging her old narrative of being unlovable.

Integrating Internal & External Receipts

While both internal and external receipts are valuable on their own, their real power comes when they're used together. Internal receipts help you reflect on your thoughts, feelings, and beliefs, while external receipts give you an outside perspective on how those beliefs align with reality. When you integrate both, you create a more accurate, balanced view of yourself and your life.

Sara deepened this practice by talking openly with Mark. Instead of keeping her fears inside, she asked him directly about his feelings and listened to his perspective. His reassurance and consistency served as external receipts, helping her align her internal fears with the truth of their marriage. This process rebuilt trust and opened healthier communication.

The following are some practical ways to integrate internal and external receipts:

Step 1: Gather the Data

Start by collecting both internal and external receipts. Internally, reflect on how you think you're doing in various areas of your life (relationships, work, personal growth). Externally, gather feedback, performance metrics, and other data points from those around you.

Sara, who struggled with overthinking in her relationship, could start by reflecting internally on her thoughts and emotions around her husband's behavior. She could then gather external receipts by having open conversations with her husband about how he perceives their relationship. The combination of internal reflection and external feedback would give her a clearer picture of the reality of their relationship.

Step 2: Compare & Contrast

Next, compare your internal receipts with the external ones you've gathered. Are they aligned, or is there a gap between how you see yourself and how others see you? This step helps you identify areas where your internal beliefs may need adjustment or validation.

Ronald might believe that his extra hours at work are having a big impact on his career. But when he compares his internal receipts (his belief that hard work equals respect) with external receipts (feedback from coworkers who see his extra hours as unnecessary), he realizes that there's a gap between his perception and reality. This insight allows Ronald to adjust his work habits and expectations.

Step 3: Adjust Accordingly

Once you've compared your internal and external receipts, it's time to make adjustments. If your internal receipts match your external ones, that's a sign that you're aligned with reality. If there are discrepancies, use feedback and evidence to recalibrate your beliefs or behaviors.

Rhonda, who'd once hoped Marcus would eventually become a responsible father, began looking outward for feedback. Her therapist reminded her how consistent she had been for Jamie. Jamie's teachers noted his sense of security came from Rhonda's reliability, not Marcus's presence. These external receipts confirmed what she already suspected—Jamie's stability rested on her actions, not on Marcus's promises.

The Dangers of Ignoring External Receipts

Ignoring external receipts can lead to self-deception, stagnation, and frustration. When we only rely on internal receipts, we risk developing an inaccurate or inflated sense of ourselves, which can cause us to make decisions that are out of alignment with reality.

There are several reasons why we might ignore external receipts:

- **Fear of Criticism:** Some people avoid feedback because they fear being criticized or judged. However, without external receipts, it's impossible to grow or improve.

- **Confirmation Bias:** We tend to seek out information that confirms what we already believe. This bias can lead us to dismiss external receipts that challenge our internal perceptions.
- **Comfort with the Status Quo:** Change is uncomfortable, and external receipts often require us to make adjustments. Some people ignore external receipts because it's easier to stay the same.

For Sara, if she'd continued to ignore her husband's reassurances and feedback, would've remained trapped in her overthinking cycle. By seeking and accepting external receipts, she was able to challenge her insecurities and rebuild trust in her marriage.

Balancing Internal & External Receipts

The key to a balanced, grounded life is regularly gathering and integrating both internal and external receipts. By doing so, you can avoid self-deception, challenge unhelpful thought patterns, and ensure that your beliefs and behaviors are in harmony with reality.

As you continue to build your receipt-based mindset, remember that both internal and external receipts are essential for personal growth and self-awareness. By embracing both, you'll create a life that's not only rooted in truth but that's also adaptable, resilient, and deeply connected to the world around you.

Now that we've examined how internal and external receipts shape our understanding, it's time to apply this mindset across all areas of life. In the next chapter, we'll dive into the practical application of receipt-based thinking across various areas, from your relationships to your career. You'll learn how to intentionally bring clarity and confidence to your everyday decisions, using receipts to guide you toward healthier, more fulfilling choices.

Chapter 10: Building Emotional Resilience Through Receipts

In the journey toward living a receipt-based life, one in which we ground our beliefs and decisions in evidence and reality, emotional resilience becomes a crucial part of the process—the ability to bounce back from challenges, setbacks, and stressors while maintaining balance and well-being. In this chapter, we'll explore how adopting a receipt-based mindset helps in building emotional resilience by focusing on reality, setting boundaries, and maintaining clarity in moments of emotional upheaval. We'll look at how to use receipts not only as a tool for decision-making but also as a resource for emotional healing, personal growth, and mental fortitude.

What Is Emotional Resilience?

Before diving into how receipts can bolster emotional resilience, it's essential to go a bit further into understanding what emotional resilience means. It isn't about avoiding pain, stress, or failure—those are inevitable parts of life. Instead, emotional resilience is about how we *recover* from those experiences. People with high emotional resilience experience difficulties like everyone else, but they have an internal toolkit that helps them respond to adversity in a way that preserves their mental health and well-being.

Emotionally resilient individuals often demonstrate:

- **Optimism:** Maintaining a positive outlook and believing that challenges can be overcome.
- **Emotional Regulation:** Managing and regulating emotions, even in difficult situations.
- **Problem-Solving Skills:** Actively working to solve problems rather than becoming overwhelmed by challenges.

132

- **Adaptability:** Remaining flexible and adjusting to new circumstances, even when life doesn't go as planned.
- **Social Support:** Seeking help when needed and maintaining strong relationships with others.

How can a receipt-based mindset—one grounded in truth, facts, and evidence—help foster these qualities? The answer lies in the clarity and confidence that comes from knowing that you're acting based on reality, not on assumptions or fears.

Using Receipts to Regulate Emotions

One of the biggest challenges we face when dealing with adversity is regulating our emotions. When things go wrong—whether it's a failed project at work, a conflict in a relationship, or an unexpected life event—it's easy to become overwhelmed by emotions such as anger, sadness, or anxiety. These emotions, while valid, can cloud our judgment and prevent us from seeing the situation as it really is.

A receipt-based mindset can help with emotional regulation by forcing us to focus on the facts rather than our emotional reactions. By asking, *Where's my receipt?* when faced with an emotionally charged situation, we create a mental pause that allows us to gather evidence before responding.

Imagine feeling hurt because a close friend didn't invite you to an important social event. Your initial emotional reaction might be to feel rejected or assume that your friend doesn't value your friendship anymore. But before you act on those emotions—perhaps by lashing out or distancing yourself—it's crucial to stop and look for objective evidence in the form of receipts. Ask yourself:

- *"Have I talked to my friend about why I wasn't invited?"*
- *"Has my friend shown other signs of disengagement from our friendship?"*

- *"Is it possible there's a reason for the exclusion that has nothing to do with our relationship?"*

By focusing on the facts, you may discover that your friend assumed you were busy or forgot to send the invitation in the chaos of planning, or that there was a specific reason (like a small guest list) for not including you. Focusing on the receipts helps you regulate your emotions and respond with understanding rather than reacting impulsively based on assumptions.

Emotional Regulation Strategy:

- **Step 1:** Recognize the emotional trigger, acknowledging your feelings without judgment.
- **Step 2:** Pause and ask, *"What am I assuming here, and where's my receipts?"*
- **Step 3:** Focus on gathering evidence to support or challenge your emotional response.
- **Step 4:** Use the evidence to shape your next steps, whether that's clarifying the situation with the other person or adjusting your expectations.

Boundaries: Protecting Emotional Energy with Receipts

Healthy boundaries are critical for emotional resilience. Without them, we end up taking on too much emotional labor, becoming overwhelmed by others' expectations, or constantly feeling drained because we haven't protected our energy. Boundaries help us define where our responsibilities end and where others begin.

A receipt-based mindset helps you maintain and enforce boundaries because it gives you concrete reasons for why those boundaries are necessary. Let's say someone in your life continually asks for favors, financial help, or emotional support without reciprocating or acknowledging your own needs. You may feel guilty about saying no. But by looking for receipts, you can clearly see the pattern of behavior and recognize that their requests are one-sided and detrimental to your well-being.

By adopting a receipt-based mindset, Ronald began asking himself, *"What proof do I have that lending money to my family makes them respect me more?"* When he examined the evidence, he realized that his family had never asked for the money—they accepted it because he offered, but their respect for him was not tied to his financial support. Ronald also applied this same receipt-based clarity at work. He realized that staying late night after night wasn't proof of commitment but a symptom of his fear of not being enough. When he asked himself, *"Where's my receipts that extra hours earn me more respect?"* the evidence was clear—his supervisors valued efficiency and results, not exhaustion. With that realization, Ronald shifted his focus from overworking to delivering quality within reasonable hours. This change strengthened his resilience, helping him measure his worth by sustainable effort rather than overextension.

Boundary-Setting Strategy:

- **Step 1:** Identify situations in which you feel drained, overwhelmed, or resentful.
- **Step 2:** Ask, *Where's my receipts?* to examine whether your assumptions about the situations are true.
- **Step 3:** Use the evidence to establish or reinforce boundaries. If you realize that lending money to family members isn't helping your relationship with them, set a boundary around financial support.
- **Step 4:** Communicate your boundaries clearly and assertively, backed by the evidence you've gathered.

Resilience Through Clarity: Accepting Reality with Receipts

One of the hallmarks of emotional resilience is the ability to accept reality, even when it's painful or different from what we'd hoped. Many people struggle with this because they're emotionally attached to a certain outcome, which leads them to deny or distort the facts. By living in a world of wishful thinking or denial, we set ourselves up for disappointment and emotional distress.

A receipt-based mindset helps us stay grounded in reality by forcing us to look at the facts, even when they challenge our desires or expectations. Acceptance doesn't mean giving up hope or settling for less—it's about acknowledging what's true and then deciding how to move forward *based on that truth.*

Rhonda clung to the belief that Marcus would eventually change. Her emotional attachment to this belief caused her significant stress and disappointment.

When Rhonda began asking, *Where's my receipts?*, she confronted the reality of Marcus's behavior—and then turned that clarity into boundaries. She stopped inviting him to events at the last minute, stopped rearranging her schedule for his convenience, and started channeling her emotional energy into creating stability for Jamie. For the first time, she was living from evidence rather than hope.

Acceptance Strategy:

- **Step 1:** Identify a situation in which you're struggling to accept reality (e.g., a relationship that isn't working or a job that isn't fulfilling).
- **Step 2:** Ask, *Where's my receipts?* to gather evidence about the situation.

- **Step 3:** Use the evidence to accept the reality of the situation, even if it's painful. Acceptance doesn't mean that you have to like the situation, but it does mean acknowledging the facts.
- **Step 4:** Create a plan for moving forward based on the reality you've accepted. This might involve setting new goals, adjusting expectations, or making changes in your life.

Resilience in Relationships: Strengthening Connections Through Receipts

Resilience isn't just about how we handle our own emotions; it's also about how we navigate relationships with others. Relationships—whether romantic, familial, or professional—can be a significant source of emotional stress or support, depending on how they're managed. By using a receipt-based mindset, you can strengthen your relationships by grounding them in truth, transparency, and mutual respect.

Using Receipts to Improve Communication

One of the most common sources of conflict in relationships is miscommunication. People often make assumptions about what others are thinking or feeling, which leads to misunderstandings and hurt feelings. By looking for receipts, you can improve communication and avoid unnecessary conflict.

When Sara started asking, *Where's my receipts?* she realized that her suspicions were unfounded. The evidence showed that Mark was a loving, faithful husband who was simply tired from work. By focusing on the facts rather than her insecurities, Sara was able to communicate more openly with Mark, which improved their relationship.

Communication Strategy:

- **Step 1:** When you feel hurt or upset in a relationship, pause and ask yourself, *Where's my receipts?*
- **Step 2:** Instead of making assumptions, gather evidence by having an open and honest conversation with the other person. If you feel like your partner is distant, ask them directly how they're feeling rather than assuming they're upset with you.
- **Step 3:** Use the evidence from the conversation to clarify misunderstandings and improve communication.

Setting Boundaries in Relationships

Boundaries are essential in relationships because they help protect your emotional well-being and ensure that both parties respect each other's needs. A receipt-based mindset can help you set boundaries by providing clear evidence of why those boundaries are necessary.

Carmen had spent most of her adult life avoiding romantic relationships because she believed that love wasn't for her. She'd convinced herself that her appearance and past experiences made her unworthy of love, which led her to push people away and build emotional walls.

When Carmen began asking herself, *Where's my receipts?*, she realized that her belief was based on fear, not reality. She'd been rejecting love before it could even happen, which led her to feel isolated and bitter. By acknowledging the truth—that her fear of rejection was holding her back—Carmen was able to set healthier boundaries in her relationships. She opened herself up to the possibility of love while maintaining boundaries that protected her emotional well-being.

This new boundary-setting gave Carmen resilience in relationships. Instead of withdrawing at the first sign of discomfort, she paused to ask for receipts. Was her fear based on evidence, or on an old wound? This practice allowed her to open up to connection while protecting her emotional energy.

Boundary-Setting Strategy:

- **Step 1:** Identify a relationship in which you feel emotionally overwhelmed or unsupported.
- **Step 2:** Ask, *Where's my receipts?* to gather evidence about the relationship. Are your needs being met? Is the relationship balanced, or is one person giving more than the other?
- **Step 3:** Use the evidence to set boundaries that protect your emotional energy. Communicate these boundaries clearly and assertively, ensuring that both parties understand and respect them.

Problem-Solving & Adaptability: Building Resilience Through Receipts

Resilience isn't just about bouncing back from setbacks—it's also about adapting to new circumstances and solving problems in creative ways. A receipt-based mindset can help you become more adaptable by encouraging you to focus on the facts and adjust your approach based on the evidence rather than clinging to old habits or assumptions.

In a professional context, Ronald believed that if he worked harder than everyone else, he'd eventually be recognized as exceptional. However, despite his efforts, Ronald felt burnt out and unappreciated.

When Ronald began looking for receipts, he realized his extra hours went unnoticed—colleagues didn't care, and his performance reviews remained unchanged. Armed with this evidence, Ronald adapted his approach. He stopped overworking himself and focused on delivering high-quality work during regular hours. This shift not only improved his work-life balance but also made him more effective and efficient in his role.

Adaptability Strategy:

- **Step 1:** When faced with a problem or challenge, ask, *Where's my receipts?* to gather evidence about what's working and what isn't.
- **Step 2:** Use the evidence to adapt your approach. If something isn't working, be willing to change your strategy based on the facts.
- **Step 3:** Stay flexible and open to new solutions, even if they differ from what you originally expected.

Building emotional resilience is an ongoing process that requires self-awareness, emotional regulation, and the ability to adapt to changing circumstances. A receipt-based mindset provides the foundation for emotional resilience by grounding your thoughts, actions, and decisions in reality. By looking for receipts, you can navigate life's challenges with clarity, Whether you're facing personal setbacks, relationship issues, or professional stress, grounding yourself in facts helps you stay resilient.

The truth may not always be comfortable, but it's the key to emotional freedom and personal growth. Through the practice of gathering receipts, you can build a life that's grounded in reality, supported by evidence, and resilient in the face of adversity.

In this chapter, we examined how building emotional resilience through receipt-based thinking can help us navigate life's challenges with a more balanced and grounded perspective. By validating our thoughts and feelings with objective evidence, we can build stronger mental and emotional fortitude.

But as we continue on this journey, it's also important to examine the relationship between trust and verification. In the next chapter, we'll explore how to strike a balance between trusting our instincts and the need to verify the information we encounter. You'll be guided in learning when to trust yourself and when to seek further evidence, empowering you to make decisions that are both resilient and rooted in truth.

Chapter 11: The Balance Between Trust & Verification: When to Trust Your Gut

When living a receipt-based life, it's easy to fall into the trap of believing that every thought or decision must be verified through external receipts. But what about intuition—the *gut feeling* we all experience? Can you trust it while still relying on evidence and rational decision-making? The answer is yes: the key is balancing intuition with verification. This chapter explores how to strike that balance by understanding when to trust your intuition and when it needs to be checked against external receipts.

To fully appreciate the role of intuition in decision-making, it's helpful to understand the neuroscience behind how our brains process information. By diving into the mechanisms of both rational and emotional thinking, we can gain a clearer understanding of how to blend instinct with evidence-based reasoning.

The Nature of Gut Instincts

Gut *instincts* are immediate, automatic judgments that feel as though they come from deep within us—hence the term *gut feeling*. But what are they really?

From a scientific perspective, gut instincts aren't mystical forces—they're the result of the brain's ability to process information quickly using past experiences, memories, and patterns to make snap judgments. This fast processing happens in the limbic system, a part of the brain responsible for emotional responses. While the limbic system can provide valuable insights, especially in situations where time is limited or emotional understanding is key, it doesn't always provide the full picture.

Gut instincts often draw on implicit knowledge—information you've absorbed over time but may not consciously remember. If you've worked in a specific field for many years, your gut instinct may guide you toward a sound decision based on a wealth of subconscious experience. However, gut feelings can also be influenced by emotional biases, fear, and prior trauma, all of which can distort the truth and lead to poor decision-making.

Thus, gut instincts can be both powerful and fallible. The challenge is learning when to trust them and when to verify them with external receipts.

The Neuroscience of Decision-Making: Emotion vs. Reason

Decision-making relies on two primary systems: rational (cognitive) and emotional (limbic). They work together but play distinct roles:

- **Rational Processing (Cognitive):** This system, controlled by the prefrontal cortex, is responsible for logical thinking, planning, and problem-solving. It takes time to analyze information, weigh the pros and cons, and consider the consequences of a decision. It's slow but thorough.
- **Emotional Processing (Limbic):** The limbic system is much faster than the prefrontal cortex. It processes emotions, gut feelings, and instincts based on past experiences. This system can generate a "fight or flight" response—especially in stressful or urgent situations—and allows you to make rapid decisions without overthinking.

How the Two Systems Interact:

These two systems work in tandem, though they can sometimes conflict. In many cases, emotional processing helps us make decisions quickly in situations where rational analysis would take too long. For instance, if you're crossing the street and see a car speeding toward you, your emotional brain reacts before your rational brain has time to process the danger.

However, emotional decision-making isn't always accurate, especially in complex situations in which more information is needed. The rational brain, while slower, helps verify whether an emotional response is valid or whether more evidence is needed before making a final decision.

This balance between rational and emotional processing is at the heart of the "trust but verify" approach. Gut instincts can be useful in the moment, but they're most effective when backed up by objective evidence.

When to Trust Your Gut

Gut instincts can be incredibly useful in certain situations, particularly when they're grounded in experience or when there's limited time to make a decision. Let's look at some scenarios in which you can often trust your gut:

When You Have Expertise or Experience

If you've been in a particular field or situation long enough, your gut instincts are often informed by years of accumulated knowledge. Your subconscious mind processes patterns and signals that your conscious mind may not be fully aware of. In these cases, your gut feelings may reflect a deep well of knowledge and experience that's hard to articulate but still reliable.

A seasoned emergency room nurse might instinctively know when a patient's condition is about to deteriorate, even before clear medical signs appear. This gut feeling is based on years of experience observing subtle patterns in patients' behavior and symptoms.

When Immediate Action Is Required

In high-pressure situations in which there's no time for careful analysis, gut instincts are often the best guide. These instincts are designed to protect you in situations of urgency or danger.

If you're hiking and suddenly encounter a wild animal, your gut instinct may tell you to stay still or slowly back away. This instinct is a survival mechanism, helping you avoid danger without needing to think through every possible scenario.

When You're Dealing with Interpersonal Dynamics

Gut feelings can be particularly useful in situations involving interpersonal relationships. Often, your intuition picks up on subtle non-verbal cues, body language, or tone of voice that your rational mind might miss. These emotional signals can help you navigate social interactions and detect when something feels "off."

If you're in a business meeting and a colleague's body language seems defensive or closed off, your gut may signal that they're not on board. In reality, your intuition is likely reading cues your conscious mind hasn't fully processed.

Learning to trust your gut is a powerful step toward self-awareness—but even instinct benefits from examination. Before you act on a gut feeling, it's important to ask: *Where is this feeling coming from? Is it rooted in experience, or is it clouded by fear, insecurity, or unresolved emotion?*

This is where a gut check becomes essential. Like reviewing internal receipts, a gut check helps you assess whether your instinct is signaling real insight—or reacting to something from the past. The following worksheet is designed to walk you through this reflection process, helping you separate intuition from assumption.

Exercise: Gut Check Worksheet

- **Purpose**: To learn how to balance your gut instinct with external verification.
- **Activity**: Reflect on a time when you trusted your instincts. Your prompts can include:
    - *What decision did I make based on my gut feeling?*
    - *Did I verify my decision with evidence afterward, or did I ignore the need for verification?*
    - *In hindsight, was my gut correct, and how could I have better balanced trust and verification?*

A gut check isn't about distrusting yourself—it's about honoring both instinct and intelligence. Each pause to reflect builds internal trust making you less reactive and more intentional. The pause allows you to draw from emotional wisdom while keeping decisions rooted in truth.

When to Verify with External Receipts

While gut instincts can be valuable, there are times when they need to be checked against objective evidence. Relying solely on intuition can lead to poor decisions, especially if emotions like fear, insecurity, or bias are clouding your judgment. Below are some scenarios in which external receipts are essential:

When Making Important or Complex Decisions

For significant decisions—such as choosing a career path, buying a house, or making a financial investment—it's important to verify your gut feelings with objective data. These decisions often have long-term consequences, and relying on intuition alone can lead to costly mistakes.

Imagine you're considering a job offer that seems exciting at first glance. Your gut tells you that it's the right move, but before accepting, it's important to gather external receipts. What's the company's reputation? What do current employees say about the work culture? Does the salary and benefits package align with your financial goals? By verifying your gut feeling with concrete data, you can make a more informed choice.

When Emotional Biases May Be Involved

Emotions like fear, jealousy, or insecurity can distort gut feelings, making it difficult to separate intuition from emotional bias. In these cases, it's essential to pause and gather external receipts to ensure that your decision is grounded in reality rather than driven by unresolved emotions.

Sara often suspected that her husband was being unfaithful, based purely on her emotional insecurities. Had she relied solely on her gut instinct, she would've believed these fears without question. However, when she sought external receipts—like her husband's consistent affection, transparency, and communication—she realized that her gut feeling was driven by fear, not facts.

Sara learned that intuition without verification led her into fear. But when she paired her gut with receipts, she found balance. Her instincts told her to worry when Mark seemed distant, but the receipts—his actions, his commitment, his honesty—showed otherwise. Trusting her gut but verifying with evidence taught her to differentiate between fear-driven feelings and reality

When Past Trauma or Negative Experiences Are Influencing Your Judgment

Psychological wounds or distress from the past can heavily influence gut instincts in the present. If your intuition is shaped by unresolved trauma, it may push you to make decisions that are more about self-protection than reality. In these cases, verifying your gut feeling with external receipts is crucial for making healthy, informed decisions.

Carmen's gut told her to avoid dating altogether, convinced that rejection was inevitable. But when she verified those instincts against receipts—positive feedback from friends, dates who enjoyed her company, and her own track record of meaningful friendships—she saw her intuition was clouded by old fears. Balancing instinct with evidence allowed Carmen to give relationships a fair chance instead of rejecting them prematurely.

Balancing Intuition & Verification

So, how do you balance the two? When should you trust your gut, and when should you verify with external receipts? The answer lies in blending instinct with evidence. The following are steps to achieve that balance:

Step 1: Pause & Acknowledge Your Gut Feeling

When a gut feeling arises, don't dismiss it right away—take a moment to acknowledge it. This helps you stay connected to your intuition without letting it completely take over your decision-making process.

Step 2: Assess the Situation

Next, consider the context of the decision. Is this a situation in which you have expertise or experience? Is immediate action required? Or is this a complex decision for which external receipts are needed to ensure accuracy?

Step 3: Gather Objective Evidence

If the situation calls for it, gather external receipts to validate or challenge your gut feeling. Seek data, feedback, or evidence that supports a clearer decision.

Step 4: Make a Decision Based on Both Intuition & Facts

Once you've gathered both internal and external receipts, make your decision based on a combination of your gut instincts and objective evidence. This integrated approach allows you to trust your intuition while ensuring that it's based on reality.

Trusting your gut and verifying your beliefs aren't mutually exclusive practices—they work best when used together. Gut instincts are powerful, especially in situations where experience, time pressure, or emotional intelligence play a role. However, in complex or emotionally charged situations, external receipts provide the clarity and grounding needed to make informed decisions.

By balancing intuition with objective verification, you can navigate life with greater confidence, knowing that your decisions are informed by both instinct and evidence. This balance allows you to live authentically, avoid self-deception, and stay grounded in reality while still trusting the wisdom that comes from within.

Where's My Receipts?

This chapter explored the delicate balance between trusting our guts and verifying our beliefs with external receipts. Trusting intuition while also rooting our decisions in objective evidence allows us to move through life with greater confidence. Now that we've learned how to strike this balance, it's time to expand our view. In the following chapter, we'll explore how shifting our perspectives—seeing situations through different lenses—can unlock deeper truths and broaden our understanding, leading to even more empowered decisions.

Chapter 12: The Power of Perspective

In a receipt-based life, truth is often found not just by looking harder at the evidence but also by changing how we look at it. Sometimes, when we're stuck in a particular mindset or belief, it can feel like we've already collected all the receipts—but often we're only seeing part of the picture. This chapter explores the importance of shifting perspectives, seeking advice and input from others, and learning how to ask the kinds of questions that open up new possibilities. Through these techniques, we can uncover hidden truths and broaden our understanding of both ourselves and the world.

Shifting Perspectives to See the Full Picture

We all have natural biases, assumptions, and limited views of the world based on our experiences, upbringing, and environment. These factors influence how we interpret information and make decisions. A shifting perspective is about stepping outside of your usual way of thinking to see things from different angles. This broader view often reveals important details or truths that were previously hidden.

Why Our Default Perspective Can Be Limiting

Our default perspective is shaped by experiences, emotions, and cognitive biases. For example, someone who has faced repeated betrayal may default to distrust, viewing all relationships through suspicion. While this perspective might feel justified based on past experiences, it limits the ability to see new relationships clearly and objectively.

Similarly, when we're emotionally attached to an outcome, we tend to filter information in ways that confirm our desires or fears. As we've covered earlier, this is known as confirmation bias—the tendency to favor information that supports our pre-existing beliefs and ignore or downplay evidence that contradicts them.

How Shifting Perspectives Can Uncover Hidden Truths

By actively shifting your perspective, you open yourself up to new possibilities and interpretations. This process allows you to challenge your assumptions, see the broader context, and discover aspects of a situation that you may have overlooked.

Rhonda had once been emotionally invested in the idea that Marcus would eventually become a reliable co-parent. But by shifting her perspective—viewing the situation through Jamie's eyes—she saw the truth differently. Jamie didn't need Marcus's empty promises; he needed one consistent, grounded parent. Through this lens, Rhonda no longer judged herself by Marcus's absence but by the secure home she was building for her son.

Strategies for Shifting Your Perspective

- **Put Yourself in Someone Else's Shoes:** One of the most effective ways to shift your perspective is to imagine how the situation looks from another person's point of view. How might they see things differently based on their experiences, values, or goals?
- **Adopt a Third Person View:** Try stepping outside the situation entirely and imagining how an impartial observer would interpret it. This technique helps create distance from your emotions, allowing you to see the situation with more objectivity.
- **Consider the Opposite:** If you're strongly convinced of one perspective, challenge yourself by considering the opposite. What evidence would support a different
-

interpretation? This exercise helps you avoid confirmation bias and opens up alternative ways of thinking.

The Value of Seeking Advice & Outside Input

While self-reflection and personal insight are important, sometimes we can only gain full clarity by seeking advice and input from others. Outside perspectives can help us see things we might miss on our own, especially when we're too emotionally involved in a situation.

Why Outside Input Is Essential

- **Reduces Bias:** Others can provide a more objective view of a situation because they're not emotionally entangled in it. They can see things clearly without the cloud of personal investment that often blinds us to important details.
- **Offers New Insights:** People with different experiences, backgrounds, or expertise can offer perspectives that you may not have considered. These fresh perspectives can open up new ways of thinking and help you solve problems more effectively.
- **Challenges Your Blind Spots:** We all have blind spots—areas of our lives or in our ways of thinking where we lack awareness. Outside input helps identify these blind spots, pushing you to confront aspects of a situation that you may have been ignoring or minimizing.

For Ronald, after seeking advice from a mentor he learned that his coworkers didn't view his long hours as impressive; some even saw them as insecurity. This outside input helped Ronald realize that his belief was based on internal fears, not external reality, allowing him to adjust his work habits accordingly.

How to Seek & Interpret Outside Input

- **Choose the Right People:** Not all advice is equally valuable. Seek input from those who have the experience, knowledge, or objectivity needed to provide meaningful insights. These may include mentors, friends, family members, or professionals in your field.
- **Be Open to Feedback:** When you seek outside input, be prepared to hear things that may challenge your current beliefs or preferences. See feedback as an opportunity to learn, even when it's difficult to hear.
- **Compare with Internal Receipts:** Once you've gathered outside input, compare it to your internal receipts. Does the feedback align with your internal beliefs, or does it challenge them? Use feedback to adjust your perspective but also check it against your own understanding to ensure balance.

Combining Perspective Shifts with Receipts

Perspective shifts and outside input lead to the same goal: uncovering receipts that might otherwise stay hidden. When you change how you view a situation, you gather new evidence that helps you make more informed decisions.

Here's how to integrate these techniques into your receipt-based mindset:

- **Shift Your Perspective First:** Before making a decision or forming a judgment, take time to view the situation from multiple angles. Consider how someone else might see it, or how you'd view it if you weren't emotionally involved.
- **Seek Outside Input for Additional Receipts:** Once you've reflected internally, gather external receipts by asking others for their perspective. Compare their insights

154

with your own and look for areas of alignment or discrepancy.

- **Ask Exploratory Questions:** Use open-ended questions to explore possibilities you may not have considered. This helps you dig deeper and uncover receipts that weren't immediately obvious.

Ronald's perspective also shifted when he began viewing his role at work through his colleagues' eyes. What he once saw as admirable late nights, from their perspective, looked like insecurity. By considering this outside lens, Ronald recognized that the respect he craved was never earned by exhaustion—it was earned by balanced, confident contributions. This perspective freed him to pursue growth without chasing impossible approval

The Power of Perspective in a Receipt-Based Life

Perspective is *everything* when it comes to uncovering the truth. By learning to shift your perspective, seek advice from others, and ask open-ended questions, you broaden your understanding of the world and yourself. This expanded perspective allows you to gather more comprehensive receipts, leading to better decisions, clearer insights, and deeper self-awareness.

Incorporating these techniques into a receipt-based mindset helps you avoid narrow thinking, confirmation bias, and emotional distortion. Instead, you open yourself up to a fuller, more nuanced view of reality, making it easier to align your thoughts, beliefs, and actions with the truth.

Having explored the power of shifting perspectives and seeking outside input to uncover hidden truths, we now turn to the practical application of validating our receipts in daily life. The following chapter is about turning the insights you've gained into a consistent habit that grounds every decision, relationship, and personal growth effort in evidence. As we make receipt-checking a daily practice, we'll look at how it becomes a foundation for clearer thinking, stronger decisions, and a life aligned with truth.

Chapter 13: The Practice of Validating Your Receipts

By this point, we've explored what receipts are, how to gather them, and why they're crucial for living a life grounded in truth, self-awareness, and personal growth. But understanding receipts is only half the battle—the real power comes from making receipt-checking a consistent habit that you apply in every aspect of life. This chapter will guide you through the process of integrating receipt validation into your daily routine, helping you create systems for regular self-checks, apply these skills in decisions and relationships, and explore the long-term benefits of consistent validation.

The Importance of Habitual Receipt Validation

Before diving into the specifics of how to make receipt-checking a habit, let's take a moment to understand why it's so important to incorporate this practice into your daily life. At its core, receipt validation is about ensuring that your thoughts, beliefs, actions, and decisions align with reality rather than assumptions, biases, or emotional distortions. While it's easy to check receipts occasionally, the *real* value comes when you make it a regular practice, much like exercising or eating healthy.

Why Consistency Matters

When receipt-checking becomes a habit, it functions like a mental hygiene practice—it prevents misunderstandings, emotional confusion, and the buildup of unchecked assumptions. Just as brushing once doesn't secure lifelong dental health, validating receipts in a single situation won't prevent future missteps. The mind, much like the body, requires consistent upkeep to remain sharp, balanced, and aligned with reality.

- **Consistency Prevents Cognitive Bias:** Like confirmation bias or availability bias, cognitive biases creep into our thinking slowly over time. Without regular self-checks, we risk making decisions based on false or incomplete information. Consistently validating your receipts ensures that you catch these biases before they influence major decisions.
- **Emotional Regulation:** Emotions can be powerful motivators, but they can also distort reality. When receipt-checking becomes habitual, it allows you to process emotions while still grounding yourself in the facts of a situation, reducing the chance of emotional overreaction.
- **Improved Decision-Making:** Regular receipt validation builds confidence in your decision-making because it provides a structured approach to evaluate whether your choices are based on accurate, up-to-date information.

Creating Systems for Regular Self-Checks

Developing a habit of validating receipts starts with creating a system for regular self-checks. These systems can be simple yet effective routines that remind you to pause, reflect, and gather evidence before making decisions or reacting to situations. Below, we'll explore the necessary steps you can take to build your own system for ongoing receipt validation.

Step 1: Set Time for Self-Reflection

The first step in creating a system for regular receipt validation is setting aside time for reflection. Just as you schedule meetings, workouts, or personal errands, you need to carve out time for mental self-checks. These can be daily, weekly, or even monthly, depending on what works best for you.

Daily Micro-Checks:

Spend five minutes each day, either in the morning or before bed, reflecting on your day. Ask yourself questions like:

- *What assumptions did I make today?*
- *What decisions did I base on gut feelings rather than evidence?*
- *What feedback did I receive that I should reflect upon?*

These quick reflections help you stay on top of your mental clarity and avoid falling into patterns of unchecked beliefs.

Weekly or Monthly Deep Dives:

Once a week or month, schedule a more in-depth reflection session in which you evaluate larger patterns in your thoughts, beliefs, and decisions. This could involve journaling or talking through your reflections with a trusted friend or therapist.

Sara, who used to struggle with overthinking, implemented a system of daily reflection. Each night, she spent five minutes reflecting on her interactions with her husband, focusing on moments where she might've let fear or insecurity drive her thoughts. Over time, this practice helped Sara build a healthier mindset as she regularly checked her internal assumptions against the reality of her relationship.

Step 2: Build Triggers for Self-Check Moments

One of the most effective ways to make receipt-checking a habit is by creating "triggers" or cues that remind you to pause and validate your thoughts or decisions. Triggers can be internal (emotional responses) or external (specific situations).

Internal Triggers: When you feel strong emotions—anger, fear, frustration, or anxiety— use that emotional surge as your trigger to pause and ask, *Where's my receipts?* This gives you a moment to reflect before reacting impulsively.

External Triggers: Identify common situations in which you're prone to assumptions or misjudgments, such as making a big decision, getting feedback from someone, or feeling conflicted about an event. Use these situations as external triggers to check your receipts.

Carmen, who had a long-standing belief that love wasn't possible for her, created an emotional trigger system. Whenever she started feeling insecure or rejected after a date, she used those feelings as cues to ask, *What evidence shows this person isn't interested?* By consistently questioning her emotional responses, Carmen was able to overcome her self-doubt and approach relationships more rationally.

Step 3: Use Tools to Track Progress

To reinforce the habit of receipt-checking, consider using tools to track your progress. Journaling, note-taking apps, or even habit-tracking apps can help you monitor your self-reflection and receipt-validation practice. Over time, you'll be able to see patterns in your thinking and decision-making, helping you adjust when necessary.

Ronald used a simple note-taking app to jot down moments when he felt insecure about his job performance. He reviewed these notes each week, comparing his emotional reactions to the actual feedback he'd received from his boss and coworkers. This tracking system helped Ronald see that his imposter syndrome wasn't based on reality, allowing him to build more confidence over time.

Long-Term Benefits of Consistently Validating Your Receipts

While the immediate benefits of validating your receipts are clear—improved decision-making, stronger relationships, and personal growth— the long-term benefits are deeper. Consistent validation transforms how you think, react, and approach life in the following ways:

Increased Self-Awareness

By regularly checking your assumptions, beliefs, and actions against reality, you develop a deeper understanding of your strengths, weaknesses, tendencies, and patterns. With this self-awareness comes greater control over your emotions and reactions. You're less likely to be swayed by fleeting feelings or external pressures because you have a strong foundation of internal clarity and confidence.

Better Decision-Making Over Time

As you practice receipt-validation consistently, you become more adept at gathering evidence, weighing options, and making informed choices. This skill extends beyond day-to-day decisions and can positively impact major life choices—career changes, relationships, financial decisions, and more. Over time, this leads to a life that's more aligned with your true values and goals. You're less likely to make impulsive or emotionally driven decisions, and more likely to create a life that reflects your authentic self.

Stronger Relationships Built on Trust

Relationships thrive when they're based on mutual understanding, clear communication, and trust. By validating your receipts in relationships, you build a foundation of transparency and trust. Others feel heard and respected when you take the time to gather feedback and validate your assumptions. As you consistently practice receipt-validation in your relationships, you develop deeper connections and reduce misunderstandings. This leads to healthier, more fulfilling relationships over the long term.

Resilience & Emotional Stability

Receipt-validation helps you build emotional resilience by grounding your thoughts and feelings in reality. Over time, this leads to greater emotional stability because you learn to regulate your emotions through evidence-based reflection rather than reacting impulsively. As you encounter challenges and setbacks, your habit of validating receipts allows you to recover more quickly, adjust your course, and keep moving forward with confidence.

Making Receipt-Validation a Lifelong Practice

The key to long-term success with receipt-validation is consistency. As you integrate this practice into your daily routine, it becomes second nature—it allows you to approach every aspect of life with a balanced perspective, free from the distortions of unchecked assumptions or emotional biases.

Remember, receipt-validation isn't about perfection—it's about progress, growth, and living a life that's aligned with reality. By committing to this practice, you'll continue to grow, learn, and thrive in all areas of your life.

Now that you've learned how to apply receipt-validation to your daily life—from your decision-making to your relationships—the next step is to move forward with confidence. You've built the foundations for making choices grounded in truth, but how do you carry this practice into every aspect of your life, even when challenges arise? In conclusion, you'll gain some final motivation to live consistently with the clarity and purpose that receipt-validation fosters. With these tools, you can step forward confidently—making decisions grounded in truth, integrity, and self-awareness.

Conclusion: Moving Forward with Confidence

You've acquired a powerful set of tools to navigate life with clarity and purpose. You've come to understand what it means to live a receipt-based life—one in which your decisions, beliefs, and actions are rooted in evidence, reflection, and honesty. You've learned to validate your assumptions, challenge your biases, and make decisions based on both internal and external receipts. This isn't just an intellectual exercise—it's a transformative way of living that invites you to ground yourself in truth, whether in your relationships, career, personal growth, or day-to-day decisions.

Throughout the book, you've been encouraged to look beyond surface reactions and assumptions. You've explored how cognitive biases, emotions, and our inherent desire to confirm what we already believe can lead us astray. More than diagnosing the problem, you've built tools to navigate complexity with clarity and intention.

Now it's time to take these skills forward and apply them to every aspect of your life. This conclusion empowers you to live with conviction—knowing that your choices and beliefs are supported by tangible proof. By moving forward with these practices, you'll create a life that's not only aligned with reality but also filled with purpose, authenticity, and growth.

The Journey of Receipt-Checking: A Lifelong Practice

Keep in mind that receipt-checking isn't a one-time event. It's a continuous process, and just like any other skill, it improves with practice. There will be moments when you instinctively revert to old habits—trusting assumptions or letting emotions cloud decisions. However, each time you catch yourself and ask, *Where's my receipts?*, you reinforce a new, healthier pattern of thinking.

This practice benefits not only big life decisions but also the small, everyday choices that shape your life. Whether you're navigating a challenging conversation, deciding on a career move, or reflecting on your personal goals, checking your receipts will guide you toward actions that align with your values and reflect your best self.

Remember, you're not aiming for perfection. There'll be times when you don't have all the information, or when you make a decision based on incomplete evidence. But the *real* power of receipt-checking comes from your willingness to reflect, learn, and grow from each and every experience.

Integrating Intuition & Evidence

One key takeaway is that a receipt-based life doesn't dismiss intuition or emotional intelligence. Instead, it teaches you how to balance those gut feelings with objective reality. Intuition is often the result of lived experience and can serve as a powerful guide. But, as we've learned, unchecked intuition can sometimes lead you down a path clouded by bias or emotion.

By validating instincts with external receipts—facts, feedback, and observations—you ensure decisions are not only grounded in feelings but also backed by evidence. This practice helps you navigate life with more confidence, knowing that your choices are balanced between trust in yourself and a commitment to reality.

As you move forward, carry these skills with you and continue to build upon them. The receipts are always there for you—*always*. Use them to guide your decisions, inform your beliefs, and strengthen your actions. By living a life rooted in truth, you become empowered to face the future with unwavering confidence and a deep sense of purpose.

Trust the process. Trust yourself. And trust that living a receipt-based life creates a path toward greater clarity, fulfillment, and confidence in all you do.

Epilogue

A receipt-based mindset transforms more than decision-making—it reshapes how you interact with the world. Imagine the freedom that comes with knowing that your beliefs and actions are supported by evidence. You're no longer swayed by fleeting emotions or pressured by others' opinions. Instead, you stand firm in the knowledge that your choices are grounded in truth.

This mindset builds resilience to face uncertainty without fear. Whether you're dealing with setbacks, unexpected challenges, or moments of doubt, you can return to the principles of receipt-checking to guide your next steps. In this way, the receipt-based approach becomes your compass, helping you stay on course even when the path is unclear.

So, what comes next? The practices from *Where's My Receipts?* don't end here—they're tools for every aspect of life. Every decision—big or small—becomes a chance to gather receipts, verify assumptions, and move forward with confidence.

You've now laid the groundwork for a life of greater authenticity and alignment. With each passing day as you check your internal and external receipts, you'll build a life that reflects your true values, ambitions, and strengths. This isn't just about avoiding mistakes—it's about living with purpose and integrity.

As you move forward, remember—you're equipped to handle whatever life brings. By asking the simple yet powerful question, *Where's my receipts?*, you hold yourself accountable to the truth, ensuring that your beliefs and actions are aligned with the evidence.

Ultimately, a receipt-based life means living authentically, aligning decisions with truth, and growing through reflection and learning. It's not about being perfect—it's about being committed to your personal evolution. Trust that with every receipt, you're building a foundation for an intentional, empowered life. You've done the work. You've learned the tools. Now step into the world with the confidence that comes from knowing you're living a life grounded in truth. You've got your receipts—now live with clarity, courage, and purpose.

Worksheets

Fact vs. Opinion Worksheet

This worksheet is designed to help you differentiate between facts and opinions in your thoughts and decisions. By distinguishing these, you will be able to gather the necessary receipts (evidence) to support your beliefs, grounding your actions in reality.

Step 1: Identify a Recent Belief or Thought

Think of a recent belief or thought you've had about a situation, relationship, or decision. Write it down below.

Recent Belief/Thought: _____

Step 2: Break Down the Belief into Facts and Opinions

Separate the belief into two components: the facts (verifiable, objective information) and the opinions (your interpretations, feelings, or assumptions). Write down each below.

Facts:

1. _____

2. _____

3. _____

Opinions:

1. _____

2. _____

3. _____

Step 3: Verifying the Facts

Now that you've identified the facts, think about how you can verify them. What evidence do you have that supports these facts? If you don't have enough evidence, what steps can you take to gather receipts (proof)?

Evidence for the Facts:

1. _____
2. _____
3. _____

Step 4: Reflection

Now that you've separated the facts from opinions and gathered evidence, reflect on how this changes your perspective. What did you learn from this exercise? How might you approach similar beliefs or thoughts in the future?

Reflection: _____

Mindful Journaling Worksheet

This worksheet is designed to help you reflect on times when assumptions led to negative consequences. Through mindful journaling, you'll explore these moments and identify how gathering receipts (evidence) could have changed your perspective or actions.

Step 1: Recall a Past Assumption

Think of a time when you made an assumption that later turned out to be false. Write about the situation below, explaining what assumption you made and the circumstances surrounding it.

Situation and Assumption:

_____

Step 2: Explore the Consequences

Describe the outcome of the situation. How did your assumption affect your actions or decisions? What were the short-term and long-term consequences of operating without receipts?

Outcome and Consequences:

_____

Step 3: Consider the Receipts

Think about how you could have gathered receipts before making your assumption. What evidence would have changed your perspective or decision at the time? Write down the receipts you could have sought out.

Receipts (Evidence) That Could Have Helped:

1. _____

2. _____

3. _____

Step 4: Reflection

Reflect on how this exercise has changed your understanding of assumptions and receipts. How will you approach similar situations in the future?

Reflection: _____

Cognitive Defusion Worksheet

This worksheet is designed to help you practice cognitive defusion—a technique that helps you separate yourself from unhelpful thoughts. By observing your thoughts as just mental events, rather than facts, you can reduce their emotional impact and respond more calmly to challenging situations.

Step 1: Identify a Challenging Thought

Think of a persistent or distressing thought that often comes to mind. Write it down below.

Challenging Thought: _____

Step 2: Use Cognitive Defusion to Create Distance

Repeat the thought to yourself, but this time, add the phrase "I'm having the thought that..." before it. For example, instead of saying, "I'm not good enough," say, "I'm having the thought that I'm not good enough."

Rephrased Thought: _____

Step 3: Observe the Thought Without Judgment

Now, observe the thought as just a passing mental event. How does it feel to recognize that this thought is not necessarily a fact, but simply a thought you're having? Write down your reflections.

Reflection:_____

Step 4: Reduce the Thought's Emotional Power

Repeat the rephrased thought several times, focusing on how it feels as you acknowledge it without attaching to it emotionally. Has the thought's emotional power decreased? Write down your observations.

Observations: _____

Step 5: Plan for Future Defusion Practice

Think of other recurring thoughts where cognitive defusion might help. Write them down below and plan to use this technique when these thoughts arise.

Other Recurring Thoughts:

_____

Five-Minute Rule Worksheet

This worksheet is designed to help you apply the Five-Minute Rule to limit overthinking and make quicker, evidence-based decisions. By setting a timer for five minutes, you'll gather important receipts (evidence) and make decisions without getting stuck in endless analysis.

Step 1: Identify the Issue

Choose a decision, worry, or issue you've been overthinking. Write it down below, briefly explaining the situation.

The Issue: _____

Step 2: Set a Timer for Five Minutes and Gather Evidence

Set a timer for five minutes. During this time, write down the most important pieces of evidence related to the issue. Don't try to analyze everything—just focus on gathering receipts that will help you make a decision.

Evidence:

1. _____

2. _____

3. _____

Step 3: Make a Decision or Take Action

Once the timer goes off, use the evidence you've gathered to make a decision or take action. Write down what decision you made or the action you'll take.

My Decision/Action: _____

Step 4: Reflect on the Experience

How did it feel to limit your thinking time and make a decision based on the evidence you gathered? Do you feel more confident moving forward? Write down your reflections.

Reflection: _____

Journaling for Clarity & Insight Worksheet

This worksheet is designed to help you reflect on your internal thoughts and beliefs through journaling. By regularly writing down your thoughts, you can build internal receipts that allow you to track your growth, challenge assumptions, and align your actions with your values.

Step 1: Identify a Recent Thought or Belief

Choose a thought or belief that has been on your mind recently. Write it down below, including any emotions or assumptions attached to it.

Recent Thought/Belief: _____

Step 2: Break Down the Thought with Reflection Prompts

Use the following prompts to reflect on the thought or belief and gather internal receipts about it. Write your responses below.

1. What have I been telling myself about this situation? Is it true?

Reflection: _____

2. What evidence or experiences support or contradict this belief?

Reflection: _____

3. What is one recurring thought that may not be serving me?

Reflection: _____

4. How does this belief align with my values, and in what ways might it be disconnected from them?

Reflection: _____

Step 3: Track Your Internal Growth

Over time, return to these journal entries to reflect on your growth. Have your thoughts or beliefs evolved? How have your actions changed as a result? Use this space to track your progress.

Reflection on Growth: _____

Self-Questioning Worksheet

This worksheet is designed to help you practice self-questioning—a technique that helps you challenge assumptions, clarify your beliefs, and make more informed decisions. By asking the right questions, you can uncover new perspectives and ensure your thoughts and actions are aligned with reality. Use this worksheet to dig beneath the surface and uncover the deeper truths that shape your thinking, decisions, and emotional patterns. These questions are not meant to judge—but to clarify. Be honest, be bold, and be willing to face what needs to shift.

Step 1: What beliefs am I holding onto that may no longer be true?

Example: "I'm not good enough unless I'm achieving something."

Belief I'm holding onto:

_____

Step 2: What am I avoiding confronting about myself, and why?

Example: "I avoid conflict because I fear being rejected."

My Response:

_____

Step 3: What patterns keep showing up in my life, and what are they trying to teach me?

Example: "I keep choosing emotionally unavailable people. Maybe I'm afraid of true vulnerability."

Identified pattern and lesson:

_____

Step 4: How am I contributing to the current challenges I'm facing?

Example: "I don't speak up, so my needs go unheard."

My Response:

_____

Step 5: What do I need to let go of in order to grow?

Example: "The belief that everything must be perfect before I start."

I'm letting go of:

_____

Gut Check Worksheet

This worksheet is designed to help you balance gut instincts with external receipts. By reflecting on past decisions and the role of intuition versus evidence, you can better understand when to trust your gut and when to seek external verification.

Step 1: Identify a Decision Based on Gut Instinct

Think of a recent decision you made primarily based on your gut feeling. Describe the situation and the instinctive decision you made.

Decision Based on Gut Instinct: _____

Step 2: Evaluate the Outcome

Reflect on the outcome of your gut-based decision. Did it turn out as you expected? What were the results?

Outcome of the Decision: _____

Step 3: Verify with External Receipts

Consider whether you gathered any external evidence or feedback to verify your gut instinct. If so, what receipts (evidence) did you use to support or challenge your gut feeling?

Receipts Gathered (if any): _____

Step 4: Reflect on Balancing Gut Instincts and Evidence

Now that you've reflected on the decision and gathered any receipts, consider how you might balance gut instincts with verification in the future. How can you ensure that both intuition and evidence play a role in your decision-making process?

Reflection: _____

Looking for a Therapist Who Gets It?

If this book helped you start asking for "receipts" in your life, therapy can help you find them. Virtual Peace of Mind offers telehealth counseling that meets you where you are — literally and emotionally.

Scan to learn more or schedule your first session with a therapist from the comfort of home.

www.avirtualpeaceofmind.com

admin@avirtualpeaceofmind.com | ☎ 888-663-2475